New Ways
to
Worship

THE SAINT ANDREW PRESS
EDINBURGH

First Published 1980 by
THE SAINT ANDREW PRESS
121 George Street, Edinburgh
On behalf of the Church of Scotland Committee on
Public Worship and Aids to Devotion

ISBN 0 7152 0454 8

Reprinted 1983

This book was written and compiled for the Committee on Public Worship
and Aids to Devotion by:

David Beckett (Largs)

Douglas Galbraith (Strathkinness)

Dorothy Griffiths (Melrose)

Andrew Scobie (Cardross)

Colin Williamson (Leith)

To all those who were good enough to respond to our request for material,
and whose insights are reflected at many points in the script, the Committee on Public Worship expresses grateful thanks.

Printed in Great Britain by
Clark Constable (1982) Ltd., Edinburgh

CONTENTS

PART ONE

PART TWO

ORDERS OF SERVICE

v

CONTENTS

NOTE: Hymn numbers refer to *The Church Hymnary, 3rd Edition*, (CH3).

CHAPTER ONE

The Need for a New Look at Worship

From the gallery a voice rings out during the reading of the lesson, not in protest but in participation. A buzz of prayer ascends from the pews as neighbours share in thanksgiving for what the week has brought. A young mother gives the children's address. The prophetic voice is heard in a contemporary poem. The readings include an epistle from a missionary partner. A smile, a handclasp or an embrace speak of peace for individual and for society. These are ways in which some people worship to-day. They are representative of many small but effective alterations within a traditional service.

Other new ways are more startling. Balloons released on the beach on Easter morning, daffodils passed along the pews, a children's orchestra in the organ loft, dancers in the chancel making vivid the words the people hear, a procession from church to grounds to plant and dedicate a young tree, even a love feast of crisps and apples shared by worshippers seated on a cathedral floor—all bear witness to a strong desire, both in conference and in congregation, to do full honour to God with all the imagination and devotion of which people today are capable, and with all the skill they possess.

The General Assembly of the Church of Scotland, conscious of the need for the church to take a new look at her worship, instructed the Committee on Public Worship to gather information on new forms of worship, and to advise as to how the new and the old might be mixed and matched. This book is an attempt to answer that instruction. Running through its pages is a conviction that if our public worship in the church is to be a living reality we may have to take account of changes in the thinking and the expectations of church-goers today. The pattern and idiom of worship have remained remarkably static in many parishes for the last fifty years, whereas the secular life of the worshippers has changed at a rate unprecedented in human history. We may rejoice in the changes or we may deplore them; but we cannot and must not ignore them.

Factors for Change

Changing social patterns raise questions for the church. New patterns of work clash with church timetables drawn up for a more stable society. Greater affluence and new leisure opportunities have made the week-end a 'prime time', in which worship finds tough competition. Increased mobility has dislodged the supremacy of the home parish. Many people work, relax or make family visits outside the area in which they live.

Change has also been forced from within the church, as one branch has become exposed to the practice of another. No longer is increased travel by more people necessary to pollinate change within the church. Cultures with overseas origins now flourishing in this country offer styles of worship which can, and do, influence the practice of the established churches. Also there has been a welcome increase in lay training, engendering a wider interest in matters of theology and liturgy.

The new scene in education is a specially influential factor. New practices and procedures in this field emphasise participation and the development of a person's own creative potential. Music, drama, poetry, art and dance have been retrieved from the concert hall, the stage, the expensive hardback and the gallery. Their use in the classroom, in community development, in the encounter group, has helped to bring into play under-developed parts of body and mind and spirit.

A readiness for fuller participation of this kind, however,

does not necessarily imply that people are less prepared to participate by listening, an ability upon which worship still depends. Indeed the argument that methods of presentation in television and the media have further reduced the attention span and that teaching and preaching now fall on deaf ears may be pessimistic. It would be more accurate to say that this has caused not a diminution of attention but an alteration. People are not less receptive: rather, their attention has to be won in a different way. Indeed there is a greater expectation now of professionalism, polish and style.

Underlying these factors is what J. G. Davies calls 'the passage from the sacral to the secular universe'. No longer does man seek divine aid to co-exist with nature. To many people nature seems capable of explanation in terms of itself, and society is examinable by human disciplines. No longer does a community turn to the church for spiritual support in a world whose workings and forces are not properly understood. Nor does it look to the church for its welfare needs. Many people of our generation do not share the presuppositions out of which traditional worship flowed. There is still in the popular mind an unhappy division between scientific and religious truth; and this division has eaten into the capital of religious belief from which an individual derived and developed his own convictions. Christian belief does not now receive confirmation from the climate of thought in society as a whole; and traditional formulations seem to ask the would-be-worshipper to ignore much of what he knows or feels. The consequences are enormous; but the least that can be said is that worship today must take account of people's uncertainties and questionings, as well as reflecting what they can and do affirm. The search for new ways to worship has a cause far deeper than dissatisfaction with language and forms.

No Counsel of Despair

The debate on the 'crisis of worship' identified by the World Council of Churches Conference at Uppsala in 1968 as a symptom of a 'crisis of faith' has not been solely a wringing of hands over dwindling numbers. There has been also a realisation of new opportunities for worship, and indeed of a new demand. Often new forms have arisen from the way the church has responded to new situations, recognising opportunities for worship in new settings—industrial, small groups, the lunch hour, conferences, communal breakfasts, and services from dawn to midnight.

The crisps and the apples, the dances and the daffodils, the poetry and the posters, have not at their best been attempts to shore up a crumbling structure of language or of stone, but a response to and an expression of a new spirituality. It is a spirituality found not just among the young, not just in one pocket of the church, but in impulses and movements which stretch across the age band, and spill over denominational boundaries. Whether these developments occur in the established Protestant churches, in the charismatic movement, among Evangelicals or in Catholic renewal, they all have a great deal in common, and are often closer to each other than to their parent traditions.

What we offer in this book is an attempt to chart this movement, to capture some of the straws in the wind. We have tried also to convey the experience of those who have sought to introduce new ways in their own congregations—to describe how they have gone about it, and what the response has been.

Not all that is included will be of use to all congregations. In particular, the complete services in the second part of the book may do no more than help share the excitement in the lives of certain congregations. Some may give shape to impulses that are beginning to be felt in the reader's own situation. A few may be used more or less as they stand. More direct assistance may be found in Chapter Four, where innovations and recoveries have been isolated and described in relation to each step in a service of worship. Those who have not yet ventured outside the traditional forms and language may find something of interest there.

Exploration of new forms of worship may bring an unexpected bonus. Two disturbing trends have caused concern at Presbyteries and General Assemblies for the past ten years. One has been the increasing number of people lapsing from active membership. The other has been the number of children who attend our Sunday Schools but never become communicant members of the church. It would be facile to suggest that these trends could be reversed by tinkering with forms of worship. It would be just as facile for the church to blame external forces for the loss of souls entrusted to us, without asking whether our own structures and traditions have become a stumbling block. There can be no spiritual health in any church whose worship has grown stale—any more than there can be real spiritual health in any church which is unrelated to the life of the community. We are convinced that greater variety and flexibility in worship are needed for tomorrow's church; and we urge ministers, elders and members to consider whether the pattern in their congregation is best suited to God's people in their parish, and their children.

CHAPTER TWO

The Permanent Factors in Christian Worship

Christ's cause in Scotland will be greatly damaged if the quest for revitalised worship becomes a source of division in the Kirk. We must always recognise the richness of diversity, the freedom we are given in Christ. There is no one proper way to worship; and we are not justified in criticising any worship medium because we do not find it personally congenial. Worship that is offered to the Father, through Christ, both in Spirit and in truth, is valid Christian worship. It is wrong to under-estimate the very real value that so many still do find in our inherited minister-centred pattern. It is likewise wrong to label all attempts at innovation 'gimmicky' or 'trendy', as if they were by definition insincere.

It is not easy to find any clear pattern linking forms of worship with particular theological standpoints. Many who would be considered theologically liberal are conservative in the structuring of worship; while supporters of doctrinal orthodoxy are often urgently seeking new ways for the church to express her faith. There is perhaps a danger though, inherent in the very concept of experimental worship—a danger that relevance or novelty may become as much of a fetish for the innovator as correctness is for the liturgist. Jesus Christ is the same yesterday, today and for ever; yet he is the Lord who makes all things new. These two truths must always be held in balance, whatever means we use to worship him.

The Nature of Worship

We believe that Christian worship is the church's acknowledgement of God, and a means of communication between God and his people. It is one of the means by which the church fulfils her witness, although it is not (in the context of a congregation's life) primarily a missionary activity. It is one of the means by which the people of God are nourished, through Word and Sacrament; but it is not primarily a functional activity devised for the sake of the worshippers. At the heart of all true worship there is adoration—the enjoyment and glorification of God for himself alone. Man's chief end *is* to glorify God and enjoy him for ever. When the whole human race has arrived at the recognition of Christ as Lord, and there is no longer any need for mission, there will still be a need for worship, the homage paid to the Creator by his creatures.

Our worship in church derives its reality and value from the power of the Holy Spirit. Furthermore, it is never the isolated act of one congregation alone. Our worship is addressed to God 'through Jesus Christ our Lord'—and in Christ we are brought into communion with the whole church, both on earth and in heaven. We are engaging in a far bigger and more fundamental activity than we are likely, subjectively, to be aware of. Worship is being offered to God continually and eternally. What we do when we 'go to church' is to join in that worship and identify ourselves with it.

For those responsible for the conduct of worship, this means that it is quite essential to help the worshippers see beyond the figure in the pulpit—or the children in the tableau or the dancers in the aisles—to the presence and reality of God himself. The parties in worship are God and his people, not the minister and the congregation. A service that leaves people thinking how ingenious the minister is has been a failure. In worship as we have known it traditionally in Scotland, the minister's task is to mediate the Word of God to his people, and to voice on the people's behalf the prayers and hopes and aspirations that they wish to lay before God. In that sense the minister's role is both prophetic and priestly—although there is no question of his acting or speaking as a representative substitute for the people. The church *is* the people, and it is the people's prayers that should be vocalised by the minister, acting as their mouthpiece.

It follows that in the preparation of worship, although God must be central, consideration of the congregation also is important. The most beautiful prayers and most cherished liturgies are of little value to a congregation who cannot identify with them—just as the most able exposition or ecstatic preaching of the Word has little value if it strikes no chord in the understanding or experience of those who hear it. Worship must be grounded and earthed in the human dimension, as well as reaching out into the dimension of eternity. It should be structured in a way that will help the members of a congregation to fulfil with Christ their royal priesthood.

The 'New Form' given to us by Christ

The most distinctive Christian expression of worship is the Sacrament of the Lord's Supper. This is one service where we have in Scripture the outlines of a given form. We stand by the view often expressed by the Church of Scotland's Committee on Public Worship and Aids to Devotion that the restoration of the Sacrament as a normal Sunday service would be a significant step towards the revitalising of Scottish worship. The Lord's Supper involves movement, participation, sharing, touching, tasting—the very elements, in fact, which experimental worship generally seeks to incorporate. Those who are seeking to move away from minister-centred worship because they feel it asks only passive involvement from church members might consider whether we have not already 'received of the Lord' the very answer to the need they are expressing.

Whatever liturgical vehicle we use for our worship, it is only the Spirit who can breathe life into it and give it any true reality. There is no way we can manipulate the Holy Spirit, but we can obstruct him if we are not open and receptive. There should be a note of joy, expectancy and spaciousness in Christian worship; and this cannot be contrived by ingenious ideas, any more than it can be ensured by fastidious adherence to ancient liturgies. We need the living Spirit to identify himself with what Paul called our 'inarticulate groans'. Everything that follows in this book has been produced in the conviction that the acknowledgement of our own bankruptcy, and sincere prayer for the illumination of the Spirit, are more vital to the church's worship than any preoccupation with forms or techniques.

CHAPTER THREE

Planning for Change

The Need for Education

It is important that members of a congregation should understand and appreciate the reasons for any changes in their services. They will be best fitted to do this when they have some general understanding of the nature of worship, and of the developing pattern of worship in their own and other traditions. Where people lack such an understanding, they are the more likely to show a rigid loyalty to familiar forms. With even a little background knowledge, people will realise that the order of service most commonly used in the Church of Scotland today is not sacrosanct. Equally, they will realise that there have been—and should continue to be—distinctive emphases. Most people, if they read *Four Centuries of Scottish Worship* by J. M. Ross, or *The Church in Victorian Scotland* by Drummond and Bulloch (p. 178ff.), would be surprised to discover how much Scottish worship has already altered over the years.

An important long-term preparation, therefore, would be to provide opportunities within the ongoing life of a congregation for members to learn about worship. At present this happens very little. There is a serious liturgical illiteracy in the Church of Scotland. A course of sermons on worship would be useful—not as an attempt to 'soften up' people before the introduction of something new, but as part of the regular provision of background information. There is need to include 'worship' in the adult education programmes of our congregations. Some teaching can be done through sermons, although it is almost more important that other opportunities should be taken (for example at Bible Study, Woman's Guild, Youth Fellowship) to increase understanding of the place and form of worship.

Resources for such groups include: *Issues for the Church, Number 2—Worship,* St. Andrew Press 1973; *Learning Together about Christian Worship,* Committee on Public Worship and Aids to Devotion 1974. It may be found that those hardest to convince of the value of fresh ideas in worship are the middle age group. Young people are flexible and ready for change. The elderly have seen many changes already and will often show tolerance of yet more, for they have proved the eternal truths in their experience. The middle age group often feel that what they have received they must preserve unaltered as far as possible for their children's sake. Regular teaching about worship is therefore a necessary preparation for any development.

The Need for Consultation

When particular changes in a congregation's services are being considered, there should be a proper process of consultation. The situation must certainly be avoided where people find something being foisted on them unawares. The aim of consultation is not just to persuade, but to allow a real partnership between minister and people in the planning and development of worship.

The Kirk Session should be involved at an early stage. It is true that the minister is ordained to lead worship, but the session as a body has spiritual oversight of the congregation. It would be not only cavalier but shortsighted to ignore its views. By consultation with the elders, it is possible to take the temperature regularly.

A number of people have had a traditional role in our worship, and they must be considered when changes are contemplated. The organist is entitled to be consulted on all music to be used. Even when a range of music is involved—guitars, recorders, stereo systems—organists should be part of the planning team. Some, indeed, are more versatile in instruments and types of music than their ministers have realised. The choir can be of invaluable assistance if they too are involved at an early stage of

planning. It is last minute directives from on high which
irritate. Choirs can help not only with musical items, but
with responsive reading and with leading the congregation
in whatever movement or activity the order requires. Also
the beadle, who has rightly regarded his pattern of duties as
important, can be an ally when these patterns are changed,
if he is put in the picture well in advance.

The worshippers too must be properly consulted and
informed—both in advance of any changes and also at the
time of a service. If a duplicator is available, it will be found
that a hand-out is a most important aid to communication
between leaders and other worshippers. Where a new element is to be introduced, an explanation on paper given at
the door allows the worshipper to prepare, and provides
something to take away for further thought. Where whole
services are of an experimental nature, an order of service
should be provided. Leaders must remember that it will not
always be obvious to everyone how the various parts of the
service relate and take shape. An order of service also
obviates the need for verbal explanations reminiscent of
'producer's instructions'. Any necessary guidance is better
to be written, put in the hands of the congregation, and
understood in the context of what has gone before and what
is still to come. The thoughtfully prepared order of service
is an ordnance survey map for worship.

The Value of Sharing Experience

There is value in contact between congregations. With
the increase in mobility, people today have more opportunity to attend other services and experience different forms
of worship, and this helps to broaden horizons. A planned
occasion, such as an inter-parish delegation, has been
found helpful in some areas. A delegation from one
congregation—including children, young people and
adults—can travel to the other, perhaps for the time of
normal worship or else for a special service on a Sunday
evening. There the visiting group leads worship, taking the

opportunity to construct an imaginative presentation involving participation in new forms. The visit is then reciprocated at a later date. There is value in having such a specific opportunity to experiment. People are literally treading fresh ground, and there can be much useful sharing of experience.

The Congregation's Resources

In the whole field of worship, whether traditional or experimental, the part that the minister plays is central. A minister is ordained to lead worship, and this distinctive role within the Body of Christ should not be abdicated. A minister must bring to this task enthusiasm and conviction about the value of living worship. On the other hand, ordination is not a licence to do violence to a congregation. The minister's responsibility can be fulfilled by offering help and guidance to others who may be taking part in a service. A relationship of trust between minister and people is essential. People will be much more ready to follow the guidance of one whom they have come to know and respect as their pastor. Above all, the ministry of leading worship must be subject to the Holy Spirit, and not be a self-conscious effort where the personality and ideas of the leader obtrude between Christ and the worshipper.

The local situation is an important factor in considering how patterns of worship can be developed. Possibilities will vary from place to place. Much will depend on the type of church building. In some smaller buildings the use of dialogue or discussion is a practical proposition; in others it would be necessary to have an amplification system, with microphones available where they are going to be needed. Fixed pews pose serious problems, limiting the possibilities of movement and of contact between worshippers. Sometimes seating can be moved. It may be possible to open up a chancel area or adapt the furnishing of a transept, to make them available for special services.

Consideration must always be given to the kind of ser-

vices to which a congregation has been accustomed. Some
congregations have been used to fairly informal services, in
others there has been a sacramental or liturgical emphasis.
The way of introducing new forms will depend in some
measure on the congregation's previous experience.

There should also be an assessment of the human
resources that are available within the congregation for use
in worship. Some initial encouragement may be necessary
before people realise the contribution they can make. Where
their experience has been of entirely traditional services,
they do not readily see how they can take part. But this
realisation grows when people discover for themselves the
possibilities in new forms of worship. Whether the congregation be large or small, the need is for the particular and
local potential to be discovered and channelled and used, so
that worship can be more truly the worship of the people.

The Value of Choice

Where there is more than one Sunday service, or where
this can be arranged, it is possible to offer a choice to
worshippers—with one service following a new form and
the other being more traditional. For example, in many
congregations an early service for families is held in the
summer months. This is a chance to use modern music and
experiment with informal methods. An evening service
provides similar opportunities—perhaps for a more
meditative service, with different treatment of the prayers
and of the exposition of the Word. There can, for instance,
be a time of guided meditation, with the church in semi-
darkness and the use of quiet recorded music as an aid to
reflection.

In one congregation the pattern is of two morning services each Sunday, the first planned and conducted by a
representative group (mainly of young people) and using
new forms, the other following the customary structure.
For those who wish it, the more familiar service is available.
At the same time the first service can afford to be different,

with a wise use of modern songs, recorded music, visual presentation, discussion and interview, and congregational participation. This arrangement is workable and stimulating, though it has the disadvantage of tending to divide the congregation into separate worshipping groups. It also makes it rather less easy to introduce changes to the second service, since it is being offered as an alternative to the first. It is certainly desirable to encourage people of all age groups to become familiar with both forms and to move happily between them.

Where there is only one Sunday service, changes will necessarily involve the whole congregation, and there is perhaps less scope for experiment. In some congregations a pattern has evolved of having one special service in each month, with services on the other three Sundays following a more customary pattern. This makes it possible to plan more adequately for the occasion when the service is to be following new lines. At the same time, the form used on the other three Sundays can become more flexible. This arrangement has the advantage of involving the whole congregation in the service with the new form. These occasions are usually called Family Services, with children attending the whole church service, instead of going to Sunday School. It should be clear, however, that a Family Service is as much for parents and grandparents as for children. If it is the main (or the only) act of worship for the congregation that week, it must provide adequate nourishment for the whole church family, and not take on the atmosphere of a children's occasion with grown-ups present—nor of an all-age Sunday School. A short, simple thematic service which is helpful and appropriate as a supplementary service may not be adequate on its own to meet the needs of the whole congregation. It is important that all moves towards experimental worship should represent an enrichment of what people have known previously, and not leave them with an impression that their spiritual diet has been reduced. Those whose worship is restricted to one

service each Sunday should take special care to ensure that
that service still bears the marks of fully evangelical
and catholic worship, whatever the form in which it is
expressed.

Means of Participation

In all plans for change, the basic conviction is that our
worship would be enriched by moving towards patterns
which allow much more explicit congregational participation. There always have been ways in which people could
share in a service, and could feel that the worship being
offered was their own worship. For some this sense of
sharing has come from joining silently in the prayers and
listening attentively to the readings and the sermon; for
others it has come from a time of quietness in church; and
all have been able to share vocally by joining in the psalms
and hymns. The search for new forms, though, has been
prompted by the desire for more general participation by
worshippers in the course of a whole service.

A simple beginning is for people other than the minister
to speak briefly in a service—perhaps in the form of a short
comment by the Stewardship Promoter at the time of the
offering, or of information about the wider church in the
form of the 'acts of today', or brief comments by members
on their work situation and how they see their Christian
response. These need not be prepared statements. The use
of an interview technique is direct, and probably preferable
for those not used to writing speeches.

There are various ways in which families can be involved,
particularly in Family Services. A family can be asked to
suggest a theme, or to choose hymns. The duties in a
service—readings, prayers, even the giving out of hymn
books—can be shared by different members of one family.

One congregation has explored other forms of family
involvement. A different family each week has been asked
to bring five or six objects for a Wonder Table placed in

front of the pews, objects which seem to that family worthy of a place in prayers of thanksgiving or praise. This produces a wide range of ideas. Alternatively, families are asked in turn to bring newspaper headlines, pictures or articles, with themes to be included in prayers during the service. On a blackboard at the front of the church is a large poster with an order of service, showing the different types of prayer that are offered in the course of a service. For a few moments before the start of the worship the minister discusses with the congregation where the themes for the week would most appropriately fit. Another variation has been for families to nominate one Bible character or story as the subject of the sermon. During the service, the character or story was slotted into place on a time chart running along one wall of the church.

Participation in the planning stage of a service is another possibility. One way of doing this is for a group to engage in a common programme of Bible reading and study and to meet each week with the minister to study the passage being used as the text for the following Sunday's sermon. The minister then prepares the sermon on the basis of the people's contributions. The Church of Scotland's Department of Education has conducted an experiment of this kind and has published three books designed for this use: *Who Measures the Ruler?*, *Questions Jesus Asked* and *Love in Action*. The same system can be used with any lectionary or Bible reading scheme.

A further stage is to use a group for the planning and the conduct of a service. In one congregation this is the pattern for an informal half-hour service, which is the first of two alternative morning acts of worship. The group, which serves for a month, consists of one or two members of organisations like Bible Class, Youth Fellowship, Youth Club and Sunday School teachers. They meet each week with the minister, decide on a theme, discuss how it might be explored in worship, and on the Sunday sit together at the front of the church and conduct the service. Even people who are not used to speaking in public can contribute their ideas and take part.

In the developing pattern of services, participation can be helped by the use of more varied forms of presentation and communication. Here again the simplest beginning is for members of a congregation to have more opportunity to speak. Use can be made of simple responses in prayers, or of responsive collects, or of a psalm said together.

Drama can be used—not just in the form of complete plays (Nativity or Passion plays) but by employing dramatic techniques which lift us 'out of ourselves' to become more sensitive to, or to see into, another's situation. A dialogue, even when the speakers are not acting a part, can help the congregation to feel more involved. Drama is in fact no stranger to worship. It consists of things that happen and are seen; and in this sense the Sacraments are the most significant examples of drama.

Music has for long been the principal vehicle of congregational participation. In the present day a new freedom is being discovered, through the use of a much wider range of musical styles. Modern hymns have a vitality and a relevance which complement the traditional hymns of the church. Many new hymns and songs have come into use in recent years, and congregations are able to make their own selection. In many parishes, church members have musical skills which can be employed in services. In schools children make exciting percussion music, and are taught to play quite a range of instruments. A small children's orchestra is a real possibility in many congregations, and is particularly suited to family services or special occasions. Many teenagers learn to play the guitar at some level of competence, and it is often possible to gather a small group which can accompany modern songs and hymns.

Visual elements are present in every church building, in the form of furnishings and windows and symbols. For particular occasions posters, paintings or collages may be used as talking points, as a focus for devotion, or simply as suggestive background. Here too there are often members of a congregation with skills that can be used. Where a church can be darkened—or in an evening service—a topic or a series of Bible readings can be illustrated with slides.

Interpretative dance is a medium of communication less often used in church; yet, historically, it has been an important religious activity. Dance is the use of movement, by itself or accompanied by music or words, to convey ideas or feelings. Young people in schools are again becoming accustomed to this method of expression. The simplest use in a service is for one or two people—in an open chancel area—to interpret a theme through dance or mime. Since dance speaks to the feelings as well as to the intellect, it can communicate ideas more eloquently than words, and can induce a fuller response in those who watch.

In planning worship we must have regard to the importance of order and sequence, for the worship of God is the antithesis of chaos. With helpful guidance, the process of discussing and trying new media and vehicles may have the effect of encouraging a congregation to understand the elements which have always been present in their Christian worship. Praise, penitence, proclamation, thanksgiving, intercession, oblation—components often blurred in the familiarity of the traditional service—may well be identified more clearly in future if even once they have been expressed in a different way. Those responsible for the planning of worship should always ensure that these elements are included in some form. The worshipper should be helped to recognise clearly what is being done, and why it is being done at that point in the service.

The services reproduced in the second part of this book are provided as illustrations, not as models to be copied. They do show, however, that within widely differing structures a basic shape of Approach to God, Word of God, and Response to the Word of God, can faithfully be fulfilled—whether these components are expressed in trumpet fanfares or in periods of silence.

CHAPTER FOUR

Suggestions for Different Parts of a Service

The second part of this book includes a number of outlines of complete services. It was felt to be helpful also to offer ideas for each stage in an act of worship—raw materials which can be drawn upon or adapted to suit the temper, the expectations or the needs of a particular congregation, and the resources available to it.

Here we are taking as our starting point the order of worship as outlined in *The Book of Common Order (1979)*, pages 42 and 43, in the belief that a great deal more mileage can be found in the procedures and practices already familiar to most congregations, and that we might often do things a great deal better than we generally do. Do hymns, for example, really inspire or challenge people in the way they ought? Is there a way of making prayer truly an utterance of the whole congregation? How do we present the scripture readings so that people hear and understand? How can the offerings be made more significant?

We start then from where we are and with what we already have—and indeed with what we have lost, since among the ideas listed are some which are recoveries of ancient practice. Some may be found preserved in common use in parts of our own or another denomination. Many are simple alterations in what otherwise remains a traditional style of worship. The reader may well find that only one or two ideas stand out as being appropriate in his own situation, but these might be enough to bring a service to life. We have sought to offer not just what is new, but also ways in which existing practices may be refreshed.

1 BEGINNING WORSHIP

Do people in your church *anticipate* worship, or do they merely *wait* for it to begin? In whatever mood a worshipper has left home, expectation may be aroused in the minutes which precede the opening of a service. Sadly, some of the interiors of our buildings have a negative effect, or even give rise to the wrong kind of expectation. This cannot be repaired in the short term. But what *can* be helped are untidiness: last month's magazines, out-of-date notices or unreclaimed old gloves. These give an impression of unreadiness which can affect the posture of the congregation. The minutes before worship begins are not empty.

To 'SET THE SCENE', what about . . .?

. . .*some material for meditation.* A psalm for the day, appearing as the first item on the praise board, will provide helpful devotional material—as indeed will the words of many hymns.

. . .*something to study,* like an order of service. This is specially useful when new material is to be introduced; but even on normal occasions the worshipper can be helped by a cover design based on original material, or a thought-provoking paragraph. There are several commercial firms which produce blank order-of-service sheets. Such a leaflet could also include news and intimations, a prayer for use before worship, a reminder of the place in the Christian Year, any theme to be followed, titles for the readings etc.

. . .*something to look at:* a poster or model, which could be made for the occasion and set in some conspicuous place. This could be related to the theme for the service. A large model telephone, for instance, has been used to introduce a service on communication. (Cribs after all are common at

Christmas.) A poster could bear a picture, text, slogan or headline. One series has a picture of a typical congregation at worship, with Jesus asleep in the front row.

. . .*something to listen to:* music clearly related to the worship that is to follow. Chorale preludes in Bach's time were 'worship-linked'; a contemporary equivalent could be a voluntary or improvisation based on one of the hymns to come later in the service. Alternatively, a record could be played which has a thematic connection with the service. A group of musicians can draw more positive attention than the predictable organ voluntary.

. . .*inviting people to talk to each other* as they arrive, turning the conversation to something each has to be thankful for during that week (a practice followed over a period of weeks or on one occasion only) so that a context for prayer is created.

AT THE ENTRY, why not arrange that . . .?

. . .*the congregation enters as a body,* having gathered in another area to hear or exchange church news—a leaf out of a Highland book, where the people await the minister outside the church.

. . .*the opening hymn is announced from the back of the church,* the minister entering while it is being sung, emphasising that the worship is being offered by the whole people together.

. . .*dramatic dialogue is used* to announce the theme or focus the attention. This is a practice going back to mediaeval times, when clergy—one in the chancel, two entering at the main door—made this exchange across the church at the outset:

> "Whom do you seek in the sepulchre, follow-
> ers of Christ?"
> "We seek Jesus of Nazareth who was
> crucified."
> "He is not here. He is risen, just as he foretold.
> Go and proclaim that he is risen from the
> tomb."

Thus was the occasion of the worship stated, the involvement of the congregation (who were between the speakers) increased, and expectancy enhanced. This can be adapted for other occasions, such as the Confirmation of new members.

...*the Bible is carried in while the congregation stands,* emphasising the primacy of the Word of God. The privilege of carrying in the Bible need not be confined to the beadle, but could be shared round the eldership, or even more widely.

THE FIRST WORDS SPOKEN should be carefully chosen, if the expectancy of the worshipper is to be sustained. The ringing phrase 'Let us worship God', following hard on the opening voluntary, has been widely found very adequate, preferably followed by an ungarnished announcement of the first hymn in the same tone. Other possibilities include:

—*a welcome or greeting,* either from the minister or given by congregation and minister to each other, for example:

MINISTER: In the name of Jesus Christ, welcome to you all.

PEOPLE: In Jesus' name, welcome to you.

OR

MINISTER: Grace and peace to you from God
the Father and the Lord Jesus
Christ.

PEOPLE: AMEN.

OR

MINISTER: The Lord be with you.

PEOPLE: And also with you.

—*replacing Scripture sentences on occasion* by words
from a different source. For instance, Article Four
of the Declaration of Human Rights has been used
in a service on Freedom. These could be heard
before the call to worship.

—*an extended dialogue* between leader and people, to
help establish the corporateness of the activity or
deepen the awareness of the nature of worship. One
example runs:

MINISTER: Who are you?
              Why have you come here rejoicing
              and singing? This is a fearful
              place. Here you will meet your
              God.

PEOPLE: We are men and women, boys and
              girls:
              forgiven by Christ,
              dedicated to Christ,
              made brothers and sisters by him.
              We have come to rejoice with song,
                for this is a joyful place.
              Here we meet our Father.

MINISTER: Are you worthy to come here?
              Have you been true followers of
              your Lord?

PEOPLE: We stand here confessing our
              unfaithfulness, acknowledging
              our unworthiness, but also our
              commitment, our love.

MINISTER: Then let us pray, with confidence
              and joy.

2   READING THE WORD

Scripture is rarely dull, yet its impact can be lost in the reading of it. Narrative, rhetoric, conversation, confrontation, hysteria, poetry, wit or warning can all sound the same when approached simply as selections of verses. The following suggestions are intended to highlight the importance of the Bible in our Reformed worship, and to make the scriptures sound as vivid as they are.

WHY NOT . . .?

> . . .*move to the lectern.* It is still a little-used piece of furniture in many churches—sometimes, admittedly, due to the design of the building.

> . . .*'close up' the readings and the sermon,* to lend shape to the service. This is not to rule out intervening hymns; but the custom of separating every spoken item by a sung one leads to the impression that readings are scattered at random, and detracts from their significance.

> . . .*preface the readings by announcement,* such as 'It is time to learn from God and hear his Word', indicating that the service is entering a new stage which may also include the exposition of scripture in the sermon (see *The Book of Common Order (1979),* pages 42-43). The traditional 'Hear the Word of God' may be more effectively used after the passage has been announced, immediately before the reading itself begins.

> . . .*carry the Bible,* before the reading of the Gospel, to the chancel steps, into a patch of sunlight or a spotlight.

> . . .*have another person read the lesson,* a new voice signalling a new activity. The reader should be chosen for clarity of voice rather than by virtue of office.

. . .*precede and follow the reading with silence,* setting
the passage in high relief.

. . .*have the congregation stand* while the Gospel passage is read, as in other Protestant traditions.

. . .*preface individual readings* by a short introduction,
preferably a single sentence, to summarise the
thrust of a passage and assist retention. This introduction can indicate the destination or context of
the original narrative, epistle etc.—e.g. 'Paul presents his own credentials as an apostle of Christ'.

. . .*precede the reading with an interview* with a
member who has consulted commentaries or taken
part in a Bible study group. The object of this
would be to convey background information essential to a full understanding of the passage. 'What
exactly would Zacchaeus' job entail?' 'Who was
Isaiah?' 'How would you describe the people to
whom this letter was written?'

. . .*use a modern translation,* perhaps reverting to the
older versions from time to time. If the Authorised
Version is used, consider offering a key verse as
rendered by the New English Bible or other modern version as a postscript.

. . .*retell the narrative in direct speech,* as though
through the eyes of a participant. This is probably
the way much of the Gospel narrative would have
reached the writer originally.

. . .*read the passage against the background of
recorded music,* when this will stimulate the imagination in the right direction: for instance, Genesis
1 to the opening of Haydn's Creation, John 21 to
'Morning' from Grieg's Peer Gynt Suite. Slides
may be used in a similar way.

. . .*employ a second voice,* and additional voices if

desired, for those parts that are in direct speech. If distance is involved in the narrative (e.g. the stranger on the shore in John 21), a reader may be sited in a gallery.

. . .*accompany the reading with dance, mime or tableau,* which further interpret the passage.

. . .*orchestrate the passage with sounds*—either for atmosphere or because of their place in the narrative—e.g. nails being hammered, wind noises (for Acts 2), a storm at sea simulated with detached recorder mouth pieces.

. . .*have the passage read from the body of the congregation* by a member, as a reminder that truth can come from within the body as well as through the minister.

. . .*read with conviction and expression*—assuming that the building, or the amplification system, allows the reader to employ a full range of vocal dynamic.

The following suggestions are intended to help lodge the passage in the experience of the congregation; and while this may be effective in its own right, it also prepares the way for preaching—from which the reading may be separated by other items or by style and language. These examples make it possible to involve people with different talents, who may already be giving expression to those talents in church drama group, youth club or local school.

Interrupt the reading, echoing a key phrase with contemporary examples—though this has to be done sparingly, to leave the passage intact. For example, after Luke 24:21—'We had been hoping that he was the man to liberate Israel'—insert without a pause (using two or more extra voices) 'We had been hoping that he was the man to break the bars of this prison and set us free' . . . 'That he was

the man to take away this hunger and stop my baby cry-
ing' ...'to allow us to live in our own country without fear
of arrest or humiliation' ...'to stop the bombing' ...'to
give us a job' ...'find us a home' ...'bring us peace of
mind' ....Verse 21 is taken up again by the original voice
and the reading continues. The inserted material may be
accompanied by a soft organ discord, or preceded and
followed by a soft cymbal clash.

Present the reading in conjunction with solo song. The
song should be closely connected with the narrative, but
containing an element of comment, or demonstrating the
similarity between original and present contexts. There are
many examples, including 'I come like a beggar' (Mark
2:15), 'Let's play a game' (Acts 2:3, Matthew 11:16),
'Tax Man' (Luke 18:9)—all published in *Jesus Folk,* and
recorded on *A Star Whispered.*

Precede the reading with a piece of contemporary writing.
This can open up a context for the listeners, drawing attention to topical situations which provide a parallel to the
biblical material (e.g. James Baldwin's short story, 'This
Morning, This Evening, So Soon' in *Going to meet the
Man*—and the exile in Babylon. Certain psalms might suitably be preceded by a prisoner of conscience poem e.g.
'Freedom is not for Idleness'—Georgi Vins in *Three Gen-
erations of Suffering* Hodder, 1976).

Supplement the readings with writings from the contem-
porary church. Epistles are still being written to-day (e.g.
Brother Roger's *Second Letter to the People of God,*
Bonhoeffer's *Letters and Papers from Prison,* messages
from the Presidents of the World Council of Churches,
Pentecost 1978) and the church is still making new dis-
coveries and meeting new situations. An issue of 'New
Internationalist' was devoted to 'Acts of Today' by indi-
viduals and groups, Christian and non-Christian (New
Internationalist No. 33, November 1975).

Open an envelope containing part of a Pauline let-

ter—'delivered' by one of the children. Explain that his letters, although addressed to a particular church, were circulated to other congregations, and are still circulating today.

3 PREACHING THE WORD

The following suggestions do not reflect a counsel of despair over the place of preaching. Indeed it may be that we need to regain confidence in the power of the sermon. However, the development of communication techniques in other fields, and the changing expectations and habits of attention on the part of those who listen Sunday by Sunday, prompt the exploration of alternatives. These are some that have been found helpful in various situations:

Unless it would be accoustically or visually awkward, consider using the pulpit only for the sermon.

The breaking of the sermon into two or three parts (separated by singing) has been common for some time now. Those who practise this know that there is a structural difference between a sermon intended for sectional presentation and one simply cut into pieces.

When the sermon is delivered as a whole, consider the possibly greater impact of a shorter duration.

Rather than follow reading with sermon, use the sermon to provide a context and prepare the ground for the principal reading, which then follows immediately or is included in the course of the sermon.

Follow the passage under consideration immediately by the sermon, while it is still alive in the mind.

Give a more devotional address from the lectern or other place in the midst of the people.

Have a group meet during the week to discuss the chosen passage, after which the preacher composes the sermon. The result will reflect the experience of people who are attempting to live the Gospel in varied walks of life.

Arrange for two or three leading questions to be put to the preacher in the course of the address.

During the sermon, invite a contribution from a second person whose expert knowledge or relevant experience would add to the congregation's understanding—for example a doctor, a layman in industry, someone who has worked in a Third World nation, or indeed a member of the congregation who has been asked to study the commentaries on the passage. The introduction and the resolution of this section of the sermon would have to be worked out with special care.

Have a dialogue between the preacher and someone with a known viewpoint on a matter of concern.

Invite a group which has met previously to discuss the passages to do so again in the face of the congregation, with the minister summing up at the end.

Present the material of the sermon with two voices alternately, each speaking once or more often. The script could be prepared in collaboration, or areas of treatment allocated for personal preparation.

Divide the congregation into groups for discussion, following an introduction to a passage for study. This can be done without necessarily stilting the progress of the worship.

Present material occasionally in the form of a documentary. This extract is from a sermon delivered soon after senior pupils at the local school had been making a study of pollution. The minister recalled sentences from the scripture readings, and the contemporary facts were read by three teenagers:

MINISTER: The earth is the Lord's, and all that is in it.

1:         But every year, the United States alone releases 65 million tons of carbon monoxide into the earth's atmosphere.

2:         And 23 million tons of sulphur compounds.

3:         And 15 million tons of oil and soot.

1:         And 12 million tons of dust.

2:	And 8 million tons of nitrogen.
3:	And 2 million tons of other gases.
1:	All these amounts are expected to double by the end of the century.
MINISTER:	The earth is the Lord's, and all that is in it. God blessed them and said: Be fruitful and increase. Rule over the fish and the birds and every living thing.
3:	But Scandinavian forests are being stunted because there is so much acid in the rain.
2:	Birds of prey are dying out.
1:	They absorb so much poison that their eggs are often sterile.
2:	Even Antarctic penguins are now contaminated by pesticides.
MINISTER:	The earth is the Lord's, and all that is in it.

Use dramatic dialogue sometimes, to explore the meaning of a passage. This is particularly suitable when the passage in question is narrative—for example, the conversation between Jesus and the woman at the well, the three voices representing respectively Jesus, the inward thoughts of the woman, and her own spoken words.

1:	Give me a drink.
2:	These words startle—no please, no thanks, no introduction or preliminary conversation, just a simple imperative from a thirsty traveller, a man, a stranger, a Jew. How do you deal with such a situation—by simple compliance, with stubborn refusal? Maybe a middle course would be best—ask a question.
3:	How is it that you, a Jew, ask a drink of me, a woman of Samaria?

4 THE PRAYERS

In the suggestions that follow, no attempt has been made to distinguish between types of prayer. Some have general application. A few can be adapted to types of prayer other than the one given in the example.

Use silence more. Short biddings followed by a silence may allow worshippers to bring their own experience and level of concern to bear, without it being 'talked out' by the minister.

The use of intermittent responses can greatly increase the devotional quality of a prayer, as in the following:

MINISTER: Lord, hear our prayer

PEOPLE: And let our cry come unto thee.

Or, in the following example, after prayers of confession:

MINISTER: Lord in your mercy

PEOPLE: Forgive us as we forgive others.

and

MINISTER: Lord have mercy

PEOPLE: Christ have mercy

MINISTER: Lord have mercy

Make absolution more definite and tangible, either pronounced in turn by minister and people (as in the Iona Abbey morning service) or said by minister to people—for example: 'In the name of Jesus Christ and by his authority granted in the church, I declare his gracious words of acceptance—You are forgiven—and issue again his call to discipleship—Follow me'.

Replace a prayer with sung material—for instance a hymn of confession; or, as a prayer for illumination, use the African responsive hymn, 'Come now, Holy Spirit Come' *(Leap My Soul)*.

Read a psalm responsively, minister and people verse about.

Have the congregation stand to say a prayer together (for example, St. Patrick's Breastplate) as a renewal of their own vows at a Baptism or when others are professing their faith (Hymn 402).

Guard against the desire to cover everything in prayers, particularly in prayers of intercession, where three topics may well be enough: one each of world, national and local concern.

In a prayer of intercession, select one main topic, and precede it with information or a very brief talk from a knowledgeable person, or a folk song which has bearing on the topic.

Have one or two members of the congregation prepare intercessions which they read from their place after a lead-in from the minister.

At the time of intercession, have the congregation confer with one another in small groups, to choose a topic which one (or all) of them translates into a short prayer on the spot, regardless of what other groups are doing. This produces a 'beehive' of intercession, symbolising the clamour of world need.

The reading of newspaper headlines followed by biddings or finished prayers may help in earthing prayer in the experience of the worshippers.

Ask the congregation to close their eyes for a short time, and listen to the noise of the world around them. The prayer of intercession then follows.

Make use of litanies, as in the conference worship of the World Council of Churches at Nairobi. ('Risk'—see Bibliography.)

The Language of Prayer

If we believe that worship is grounded in the human dimension and also reaches out into the dimension of eternity, the kind of language that is used in worship is of special significance. Words serve as pointers and the language of worship should be capable of this double reference. That is to say, it should be a language which honours God, and with which people can identify.

In our situation there are strong reasons for reviewing the traditional vocabulary of worship. The meanings of words change considerably, and where the original context is no longer familiar, language loses its power. When the Book of Common Prayer was written, 'naughty' meant 'wicked' and 'miserable' meant 'pitiable', but these words would conjure up for us now very different impressions from those originally intended. Customs change also in the way words are used and put together, and while the frequent use of inversion and long relative clauses may once have been appropriate, the need now is for much simpler and more direct forms of expression. The language of prayer has been much influenced by the language of the Bible—our traditional prayers contain many echoes of the Authorised Version—and the increasing use of modern translations both prompts and guides the search for an appropriate contemporary language of prayer.

The task of revision is one that requires as much skill and sensitivity as can be brought to it. Some attempts at modern prayers descend to language which is inappropriate and even banal. Care should be taken to avoid tinkering or clumsy modernising, as, for example, in the attempt to keep the content of a traditional prayer and change the grammar, simply replacing 'thou' with 'you'. In the search for intelligibility, it is important not to lose the sense of mystery, and thereby to reduce prayer to a level of functional flatness. As Stephen Spender says: "Words are an extremely difficult medium to use, and sometimes when one has spent days trying to say a thing clearly, one finds one has only said it dully". The language of worship—unlike scientific language which is used to contain and define meaning—is akin to poetic language and should be evocative as well as informative. It is a form of communication which expressed human longings and convictions and which points to a reality beyond human experience. The following opening prayer of adoration, by The Revd. Dr. E. S. P. Jones, may serve to illustrate this expansive use of language:

> 'O wind in our faces, Fire in our souls, Joy in our midst,
>   Thunder upon many waters;
> Majesty surrounding us, Steadfastness supporting us,
>   Graciousness beckoning us, Love welcoming us:
> Now is the daylight upon us and our hearts full of
>   expectancy as your promises advance upon us.
> The cities stir from slumber, the country wakens from
>   sleep, the villages arise for a new day;
> all that comes to be is alive with your life,
> and that life is the light of men.
> Blessed are you, our God, for ever and ever.'

In this prayer poetic images are very happily combined with a Biblical image from St. John's Gospel. The task is not simply that of up-dating language. Rather it is a question of identifying both old and new symbols which have the evocative power to convey to twentieth century man the mystery of God and the depth of human relationships. We have scarcely begun to use in our worship images from modern life. Yet our knowledge of subjects such as modern medicine, electricity, and nuclear physics could provide us with interesting and evocative new images. At the same time distinctive Biblical images, which belong to the given tradition of Christianity, will continue to have a rightful place in prayer. Part of the educational task of the Church must be to initiate people into an appreciation and understanding of these images. In some cases amplification or elucidation will be required. In other cases we may discover that traditional words like 'ransom' come to have additional meaning through modern associations. The former Dutch Jesuit priest Huub Oosterhuis is one person who has imaginatively explored the use in worship of terms which are concrete, personal and individual, and who has shown

that language which is down-to-earth can also have beauty
of phrase. The following short extract from his eucharistic
prayer indicates how well a word like 'covenant' can fit into
a modern context:

> 'We beseech you
> send over us your Holy Spirit
> and give a new face
> to this earth that is dear to us.
> May there be peace
> wherever people live,
> the peace that we cannot make ourselves
> and that is more powerful than all violence,
> your peace like a bond,
> a new covenant binding all people together
> in the love of Jesus Christ
> here among us.'

5 THE OFFERING

Some parishes have been accustomed to having people
place their offerings in a plate as they enter church, for
presentation at an appropriate part of the service. It is
assumed here, however, that the giving of our offering
should be a deliberate act, a response to the Word read and
preached, taking place in the latter part of the service.

Instead of having an organ voluntary, uplift the offering
in silence, prefacing the announcement by words designed
to help people become more aware of the significance of
this act.

Invite people to bring their gifts of money to the front or
to the Table in person, thus symbolically offering themselves.

Before the offering is presented, the minister says, 'If any
man remember that your brother has a grievance against
you, first go and make peace with your brother, and only
then come back and offer your gifts', followed by 'The

peace of Christ be with you', and the handshake of fellow-ship amongst the congregation.

The people can sing while the offering is gathered. An appropriate hymn from the hymn book can be used, or an African responsive hymn—which can be easily adapted to last as long as required: for example, 'His Kingdom beckons us now' *(Leap My Soul)* or 'The Poor are Served' *(Free to Serve).*

6   THE INTIMATIONS

These suggestions acknowledge that the intimations are in practice placed in a variety of positions in worship. The first question to be asked, though, is whether at present they are in the right place. Do they assist worship, or do they interrupt the flow? Given before worship begins but after the entry they may leave the ensuing service intact, but at the cost of disturbing the momentum built up by the opening music and the entry of the Bible. Taken after the congregation has responded to the Word in hymn, creed or offering, they may have some purpose in giving necessary information as the congregation prepares to bring before God the needs of his world and his church.

WHY NOT...?

. . .include items of news from the wider church, thus helping those gathered for worship towards an awareness of the church universal.

. . .include items of local news, to remind the congregation of their function in respect of their local community and parish.

. . .prepare intimations carefully as a 'script', to allow for greater clarity and impact, and to avoid over-elaboration.

. . .print intimations in an order of service instead of—or as well as—reading them during the service.

...have two voices read single items alternately, with brief pauses, to allow the details to register and to reduce the possibility of confusing one piece of information with another.

...include news of events or meetings which have already happened during the past week, as well as information about forthcoming events.

...when intimations are placed close to the prayer of intercession, end them with information about topics to be included in that prayer.

...allow for representatives to make announcements about their own organisations, and to give a personal invitation to attend.

...place the intimations in a 'gathering time', perhaps in a separate hall just prior to the beginning of worship, allowing others to contribute items in an informal atmosphere.

7   THE HYMNS

The music and the hymns of the church are of particular importance to its people, being the principal means of congregational participation. It is a subject on which most people have views, and a discussion which did it justice would fill a book of its own. However, the following suggestions may be found useful.

The five singings which are the norm in many parishes may tend to give worshippers the impression that worship is a hymn sandwich. The development of the worship may be clearer if the number is reduced to four.

Do not confine the psalms and paraphrases to the opening of a service. Many of them come more suitably at other points in the worship, particularly in association with the reading of the Word.

All items of praise should be relevant to that part of the service in which they are set, and not repeat stages through which the worship has already passed. *The Church Hymnary: Third Edition* and *A Year's Praise* are helpful in this regard as reference books for the selection of psalms and hymns.

Consider the possibility of alternative accompaniments to the organ—for example, a piano, a children's orchestra, solo instruments or unaccompanied singing. Some modern hymns, in particular, do not lend themselves to organ accompaniment.

Modern hymns may be very helpful, if introduced correctly and sung well. They reflect contemporary insights, to the general enrichment of worship, and their appeal is by no means confined to the young.

The period before worship begins may be found suitable for introducing new material. On occasion, a longer time may be given over for this purpose when hymns for a few weeks ahead are being introduced together.

Although close consultation with the organist is desirable, the responsibility for choosing hymns is the minister's. They should be related to their place in the service, to the Christian Year, and to any theme being followed.

With a wide range of modern hymns now available for worship, congregations may wish to make their own selection and print words in a duplicated booklet. Remember to seek permission to use copyright material and be prepared to meet fees if required. It may also be possible to include hymns and songs by local people.

Demonstrating new material to congregations is not necessarily part of an organist's job. A teacher with an interest in music may, among others, have the required knack.

Find out what is being sung in local schools, and what musical resources might be available to the church.

8 THE SACRAMENT

When congregations are approaching more frequent celebrations of the Lord's Supper, the ideal is for all the people to participate—so that perhaps one service each month becomes a Communion Sunday, without cards and the overtones of discipline which still accompany them.

In some situations, however, the majority within a congregation may not be anxious to have the Sacrament more frequently available; and it could be divisive to insist on a general celebration even once a month. In this case it is better to accept that there must be an opportunity for some to leave before the Sacrament. The aim must be to encourage a love of Holy Communion, and love cannot be commanded. Those who do not wish to receive communion must not be made to feel ill at ease because they leave church after the Liturgy of the Word. At the same time, those who remain must be able to recognise that the Sacrament is the climax of their morning worship, and not a separate activity tacked on to but divorced from what has gone before. The following suggestions may be helpful:

The invitation to the Lord's Table should be given during the main service.

The order of service should proceed as usual (see *The Book of Common Order (1979)*, pages 42-43) with the omission of prayers of thanksgiving and the Lord's Prayer, which may be reserved for the order of the Lord's Supper itself.

A blessing may be given, reserving words of dismissal until the conclusion of the Sacrament.

If it is the normal practice, the minister may go to the door to greet those who leave at this point. One city congregation which has an average attendance of fifty at regular communion, keeps the elements in a locked cupboard in the vestibule. When those receiving communion have gathered in the front pews and the others have left, the minister can announce the communion hymn and re-enter the church with four elders bearing the elements. In this way the continuity of the service is preserved.

Where Holy Communion follows the main diet of worship it may be wise to resist the temptation of using a side chapel or the chancel choir stalls for those who remain to communicate. The impression must not be given that the sacrament is an extra for the few. Kirk Sessions discussing the frequency of Communion may find it helpful to make use of the leaflet *Weekly Communion in the Church of Scotland*—St. Andrew Press, 1974.

9 THE ENDING

A service of worship should have a strong finish. A well chosen final hymn will make an important contribution, but consider also:

- —replacing the commonly used three-fold Amen, which has a 'dying fall' with, for instance, the more resolute and rising Dresden Amen, or a firm congregational spoken response.
- —using, before the benediction, a dismissal which bears some relation to the content of the service (see *Prayers for Contemporary Worship,* p. 89 ff.).
- —having a member of the congregation voice the dismissal, summing up the thrust of the service—e.g. 'Let us go from here and . . .' or 'Brothers and sisters, we are to . . .'.
- —following the benediction with some symbolic act on the part of the congregation (such as the planting of a tree, instanced in Chapter One).
- —continuing the occasion with a shared meal, such as breakfast after an Easter dawn service, or a Christian Aid lunch.

—a closing dialogue. This example is from the conclusion of an Easter morning service:

MINISTER: In the strength of Jesus' victory
VOICE 1:   We go from here
VOICE 2:   His messengers
VOICE 3:   His brothers

MINISTER: Commissioned to carry his love
VOICE 2:   Into every part of our daily life—
VOICE 3:   Our work
VOICE 2:   Our school
VOICE 1:   Our homes
VOICE 3: And our family life.

MINISTER: Jesus is Lord!
VOICE 2:   Not a good man now dead
VOICE 1:   But a risen Saviour;
VOICE 2:   Not a figure in a book
VOICE 3:   But a living presence with us.

MINISTER: We will worship him,
VOICE 1:   And serve him,
VOICE 3:   And trust him,
VOICE 2:   And be guided by him.

MINISTER: For he is our Lord and our God, in
           life and in death, and to all eternity.

           Now the God of peace, who
           brought again from the dead our
           Lord Jesus, that great shepherd of
           the sheep, through the blood of the
           everlasting covenant, make you
           perfect in every good work to do his
           will, working in you that which is

well pleasing in his sight. And the blessing of God Almighty, Father, Son and Holy Spirit, be upon you and remain with you always.

ALL: AMEN.

All these suggestions have this in common—that they have been tried, or are currently being practised, by some congregation somewhere. Those planning worship will use their judgement as to which require regular use for their value to be appreciated, and which make their best impact when employed only occasionally.

PART TWO

ORDERS OF SERVICE

NOTE: *The services included in this section are not intended to be the basis of a new common order in the church. They are offered as examples of different types of worship which have been found helpful in widely varying parish situations. Such services tend to derive much of their value from spontaneity and from topical relevance—qualities which are not easy to reproduce in print after an interval of months or years. This means that it will seldom be possible to reproduce any of these services exactly as it is written, at a different time in a different place; but the Committee has done very little editing, preferring to let them stand as individual contributions to the development of worship in a cross-section of the parishes of Scotland.*

A. SELECTION OF ORDERS FOR GENERAL USE

1. AN ORDER OF MORNING WORSHIP

This order is in regular use in a small rural congregation but could be used or adapted for any parish situation.

The Approach

MINISTER: In the name of the Lord Jesus Christ, welcome to you all.

PEOPLE: In Jesus' name, welcome to you.

HYMN

PRAYERS

"MARK TIME":
a short presentation with the children particularly in mind which serves as a common introduction to the theme for the day, to be pursued later in Sunday School and in sermon. In this instance, the Gospel of Mark was being examined week by week. The pattern was:

Signature tune on cassette.

Child turns next page of 'gospel', a large loose-leaf book with pictures or symbols matching the narrative.

The minister retells the story for the day.

A new verse is introduced to a recurring song, the chorus of which the children sing as they now leave the church.

The Word

MINISTER: It is time to learn from God and to hear his Word.

THE READINGS

PSALM or PARAPHRASE (or suitable HYMN)

SERMON

The Response to the Word

HYMN

NEWS AND INTIMATIONS
(Items of wider church news and of local community interest are included: information to assist prayers of intercession may also be given.)

THE OFFERINGS

PRAYERS—of Intercession, Dedication, and Lord's Prayer.

HYMN

BENEDICTION

2. AN ALTERNATIVE ORDER OF MORNING WORSHIP

The shape of this service derives from early Christian worship. It also allows the opportunity of more frequent celebration of the Sacrament of the Lord's Supper, suggesting a less formal procedure than that followed in a quarterly Communion. It is in periodic use as a family service in a village congregation.

The Entry

Worshippers gather outside church (or in the church hall) and greet each other. Hymn books are given out by the children. News and intimations are announced and shared.

MINISTER: "Acclaim the Lord, all men on earth,
worship the Lord in gladness;
enter his presence with songs of exultation."

HYMN or PSALM *(unaccompanied to begin with)*
As this is sung, all process into church, following the Bible, the organ taking up the accompaniment. The Offerings may be given as the people enter.

The Word

OLD TESTAMENT READING

EPISTLE

GOSPEL (at the conclusion of which:
MINISTER: This is the word of the Lord.
PEOPLE: Thanks be to God.)

HYMN

SERMON

HYMN
>(It may be possible, as an alternative, to present the
>material in this section in other ways—for instance, in
>a more flowing presentation of reading, comment and
>song. A children's, or simple, talk on the theme of the
>day could be included also in this section.)

The Prayers and the Peace

PRAYERS of intercession
>(This may consist of three petitions, in the
>order—church, world, local concern. These could be
>offered by members of the congregation from their
>places. Relevant information to assist prayer could be
>shared before the prayer as a whole begins.)

PRAYERS of confession and absolution
>*(said by the minister or by the whole congregation
>together)*

THE PEACE
>MINISTER: We meet in Christ's name: let us share his
>peace.
>
>ALL: Peace be with you.
>(The people greet each other with a hand-
>clasp, saying: "Peace be with you".)

The Bread and the Wine

HYMN
>(During which the offerings are presented and the
>elements brought in, in procession. During the last
>verse the congregation could make their way to the
>front pews.)

MINISTER: On the side of a hill,
>in the home of an outcast,
>on the shore of a lake,
>behind doors locked for fear,

at the end of a journey,
Jesus drew his friends around him
in the sharing of food and drink.

And most memorably of all
in the upper room
he bound their lives together with his,
when in bread and wine
he brought his kingdom to life amongst them.

READER: Matthew 26:26-29

MINISTER: Let us pray.

With heart and voice we praise you, O Lord.
All that lives owes its life to you,
brought into being by your power and love.
You have made mankind in your own image,
and stay true to all you have created.

Above all we celebrate the coming of Christ,
his life on earth and his presence today,
the cross which signals the end of slavery,
his rising which sets us free to follow him,
the sending of the Holy Spirit
to give power and purpose to the church.

As he offered himself as true man
that he might make of us a new creation,
so now we offer this bread and this wine,
fruits of the earth and signs of his sacrifice.
By the presence and the power of the Holy
Spirit,
may they become his life in us
and a foretaste of life in a world remade.

With them we offer also ourselves,
what we are and what we could become.
Upheld by a new and vivid hope
to which nothing seems too good to be true,
may we reflect in our words and actions
the One who is Lord of our lives—

Whom we acclaim in song and speech,
in sharing, movement, taste and touch.

And in his words we pray,
Our Father . . .

MINISTER: (breaking the bread and pouring out the wine)
            The body of Christ, broken for you . . .
            and his Life, poured out for our salvation.

*(Having himself/herself communicated, the minister offers
both bread and wine by passing them to his nearest neighbours. They are circulated through the congregation. If the
congregation is large, either the people come forward in
groups or elders take the elements to the people.)*

DISMISSAL AND BENEDICTION, such as the following:

God has accepted your offering in Christ;
go now to offer yourselves,
as God's people,
to the world he loves;
and the blessing of God,
Father, Son, and Holy Spirit,
be with you all.

HYMN (recessional):
the minister and elders leave church, followed by the
people.

3. AN ORDER OF EVENING WORSHIP

NOTE: *For the meditation, a microphone is used, to allow the use of a quieter tone of voice. Lights are turned off, except for the light over the Communion Table; and as part of the meditation there is an extended time of quiet music for reflection—either organ music or recorded music played over the church stereo system.*

The service includes material borrowed from the British Council of Churches 'Dayspring' conference, and from the World Council of Churches Nairobi Assembly.

ORGAN VOLUNTARY

CALL TO WORSHIP

PRAYER—of approach:

MINISTER: You are the one and only God; there is none like you, Lord.
You are great and your name is holy.
May all the glory be yours.

PEOPLE: By the worship of your church in every generation;
by the worship of our minds and hearts today;
may all the glory be yours.

MINISTER: By the proclamation of the coming of Jesus;
by our receiving him into our hearts and lives;
may all the glory be yours.

PEOPLE: By the living of our lives in faith;
by our hope in the Lord Jesus;
by the labour of our love;
may all the glory be yours.

MINISTER: By the winning of the world and the recon-
ciliation of all people;
may all the glory be yours.

PEOPLE: Holy, holy, holy, Lord God of hosts.
Heaven and earth are full of your glory;
glory be to you, O Lord most high.

HYMN of glory

PRAYER of confession, and assurance of pardon:

MINISTER: In quietness let us lay before God the burden of our sinfulness
(a time of silence)

PEOPLE: Most merciful God,
we confess that we have sinned in thought,
word and deed.
We have not loved you with our whole
heart.
We have not loved our neighbours as ourselves.
In your mercy, forgive us and restore us to
your fellowship;
that we may do justly, love mercy, and
walk humbly with you;
through Jesus Christ our Lord.

MINISTER: Christ Jesus came into the world to save
sinners.

Hear then the word of grace and the assurance of pardon to all who are truly peni-
tent: Your sins are forgiven, for his sake.

HYMN

MEDITATION WITH BIBLE READING

RECORDED MUSIC

THE APOSTLES' CREED, OR OTHER AFFIRMATION OF FAITH

EVENING HYMN

THE OFFERINGS

A TIME OF PRAYER

THE LORD'S PRAYER

CLOSING PRAYER:

MINISTER: Darkness has fallen again over the face of the abyss, covering the earth. Silence grows, movement ceases, night closes round us.

PEOPLE: Lord, darkness is no darkness to you;
to you, both dark and light are one.

MINISTER: Our dusk will be like noonday, and like dawn out of darkness our light will rise. The people that walk in darkness have seen a great light.

PEOPLE: Lord, darkness is no darkness to you;
to you, both dark and light are one.

MINISTER: Night with night shares its knowledge; and this without speech or language or sound of any voice.
Let us be still and know that God is ...
(a moment of silence)

PEOPLE: Lighten our darkness, we pray, O God, and by your great mercy defend us from all perils and dangers of this night; through Jesus Christ our Lord.

MINISTER: Lord, darkness is no darkness to you;
PEOPLE: To you, both dark and light are one.

MINISTER: As the earth keeps turning round, hurtling through space, and night falls and day breaks from land to land, let us remember people waking, sleeping, being born and dying—one world, one humanity . . .
(a moment of silence)

MINISTER: Let us go from here in peace

PEOPLE: Lord, lighten our darkness and stay with us.

ORGAN MUSIC

4. A FAMILY SERVICE ON THE THEME OF 'FAITH, HOPE, LOVE'

THE GREETING

> Minister: The Lord be with you
>
> People: And also with you.

INTIMATIONS

THE SENTENCES (said together):

> Sing to the Lord all the world. Worship the Lord with joy.
>
> Come before him with happy songs.
>
> This is the day of the Lord's victory. Let us be happy. Let us celebrate.
>
> Clap your hands for joy, all peoples. Praise God with loud songs.

SONGS:

> 'This is the day' *(Sound of Living Waters)*
>
> 'Clap your hands' *(Come Together, J. Owens)*

THE COLLECTS

SCRIPTURE READING: Exodus 14:19-25

ADDRESS

PRAYER

> (during which the congregation, remaining seated, sing verses 1 and 2 of HYMN 81—'My faith looks up to thee')

ACT OF FAITH:

> The Apostles' Creed

HYMN 472

> 'Fear not, thou faithful Christian flock'

SCRIPTURE READING
    1 Peter 1:3-9

ADDRESS

PRAYER

ACT OF HOPE: HYMN 325
    read responsively—'From glory to glory advancing,
    we praise thee, O Lord'

HYMN 411
    'My hope is built on nothing less'

SCRIPTURE READING
    John 21:15-17

HYMN 416
    'God is love: his the care'

ADDRESS

SONG
    'Love is the greatest thing'

THE OFFERINGS

ACT OF LOVE
    The handshake of peace

PRAYERS

HYMN 418
    'Jesus loves me!'

THE BLESSING

5. A SERVICE ON THE THEME OF 'LEARNING ABOUT THE CHURCH'

This family service was designed to fit in with the part of the Sunday School syllabus being studied in Sunday School at the time (Learning in the Church).

THE CHURCH IS GOD'S FAMILY

HYMN 427—'The Church is wherever God's people are praising'

IN OUR FAMILY: THE THINGS WE REMEMBER

TALK

PRAYER

HYMN 386—'Praise him, praise him, all ye little children'

IN OUR FAMILY: THE THINGS WE SAY AND DO

TALK

PRAYER

HYMN 448—'Just as I am, thine own to be'

IN OUR FAMILY: THE THINGS WE SHARE WITH OTHERS

TALK

THE OFFERINGS

PRAYER, and THE LORD'S PRAYER

HYMN 467—'Take our gifts, O loving Jesus'

THE BENEDICTION

IN OUR FAMILY: FELLOWSHIP IN THE HALL

6. A FAMILY SERVICE ON THE THEME OF 'LIGHT'

Materials: *Slide projector; glass or plastic prism (borrowed from school); disc of stiff card, 6-9 inches in diameter, marked with poster or oil paint into segments on each side corresponding to the colours of the rainbow in proper order, with two small holes pierced just on either side of centre, and centrally suspended on a loop of string—about 1 metre, depending on length of arms.*

HYMN 154
   'All things bright and beautiful'

PRAYER

SCRIPTURE READING
   Genesis 1:1-5

FIRST PART OF ADDRESS

   Explain theory of light and vision. Ask children to close their eyes. They see nothing because we only see things when they reflect light. Ask what colour light is, then show that light is made up of seven colours which can be taken apart and put together again (projector throws white beam on wall, prism bends beam and breaks it up into seven colours).

   Display disc. Spin it (having wound it tight) to show the seven colours merging together to form light. Why do we not see all objects the same colour? Because no object reflects *all* the light it receives. 'It is what you give back that shows what colour you are.'

HYMN 157
   'We thank thee, God, for eyes to see'

               OR

HYMN 465
   'Hands to work and feet to run'

SCRIPTURE READING
Genesis 28:10-22 (Jacob's Ladder)

SECOND PART OF ADDRESS
Highlight Jacob's vow to give back to God a tenth of all that God might give him. Develop in a simple way the concept of Christian Stewardship, and contrast this with the common practice of living selfishly. 'It is what you give back that shows what colour you are.'

HYMN 456
'We give thee but thine own'

OR

HYMN 467
'Take our gifts'

SCRIPTURE READING
Matthew 5:38-48 (Turning the other cheek)

THIRD PART OF ADDRESS
Brief address on Christian conduct. End with Jesus saying 'I am the light of the world', and 'You are the light of the world'. This can be true only if you reflect all that we see in him and receive from him. 'It is what you give back that shows what colour you are.'

HYMN 112
'Jesus Christ, I look to thee'

PRAYER

THE OFFERINGS

HYMN 488
'Jesus bids us shine'

OR

HYMN 95
'O light that knew no dawn'

THE BLESSING

7. A FAMILY SERVICE ON THE THEME OF 'FORGIVENESS'

This service was one of a series of summer family services held between Sunday School sessions every Sunday as an alternative to the 11 o'clock worship. Accompaniment for the hymns was provided by a group of teenagers playing piano, violins, oboes, guitars, trumpet and trombone.

CALL TO WORSHIP

HYMN
'Thank you for every new good morning' *(Youth Praise,* Vol. 1)

PRAYERS
of approach and supplication

ADDRESS
explaining the centrality to the Gospel of forgiveness, and pointing out that the element of confession was left out of the first prayer—deliberately.

Paper and pencils were handed round, and the congregation were asked to spend a few moments writing down the sins of omission and commission that they had to confess from the previous week—also any people we had hurt, neglected etc. This was followed by a short period of silence for private prayer.

The congregation were then asked to fold their papers and pass them to the end of the pews, where the minister collected them in the offering plate, before laying them on the Table—the record of all our ugliness and disobedience during the previous week.

The papers were then tipped on to a barbecue in front of the Table, and set alight. While they were burning, the minister read some of the scriptural promises of forgiveness:

Come now, let us reason together, says the Lord. Though your sins are scarlet, they may become white as snow; though they are dyed crimson, they may yet be like wool.

Blessed be the Lord God of Israel, for he has visited and redeemed his people.

The words of Jesus:

Come unto me, all ye that labour and are heavy laden, and I will give you rest.

Peace I leave with you.

I am not come to call the righteous, but the sinners.

I have come into the world as light, so that no-one who has faith in me should remain in darkness.

Go in peace; your sins are forgiven.

There will be greater joy in heaven over one sinner who repents than over ninety-nine righteous people who do not need to repent.

HYMN
'There is joy among the angels' *(Youth Praise,* Vol. II)

THE OFFERINGS

PRAYERS of thanksgiving, intercession, dedication; and the Lord's Prayer

HYMN
'Only Jesus' *(Youth Praise,* Vol. II)

THE BLESSING

8. A SERIES ON THE THEME OF 'OUR SENSES'

The following examples are from a series of informal summer family services which centred each week on different senses—on things that are hard to say, see, do, understand, hear, feel, taste and believe. There was opportunity in each of the services to use the relevant senses. This provided a variety of different kinds of participation, and the subjects allowed reference to a wide range of biblical material. The order of the service varied little, and followed a general pattern of Approach to God, God's Word, and Response to God's Word. The thematic presentations provided a context within which the Bible reading was shown to be relevant.

(A) SPEAKING

WELCOME AND INTRODUCTION

SONG
    'Standing in the need of prayer'

PRAYER of approach to God, said together:

MINISTER: We worship you, Lord God

PEOPLE: We call you by human names and words

MINISTER: But no names or words can encompass you. You are God—beyond the reach of language and imagination.

PEOPLE: Yet we pray to you; we open our hearts to receive you and your word.

MINISTER: Attune us to your voice

PEOPLE: And to your silence.

MINISTER: Today is the day that we are called together

PEOPLE:	To be your church and celebrate your presence.
MINISTER:	We are glad to be here to-day,
PEOPLE:	Linked with the great family of Christians around the world,
MINISTER:	Companions in worship, sharers of a common faith
PEOPLE:	In Jesus Christ our Lord.

SONG
'Rejoice in the Lord'

BIBLE READING

ADDRESS: Tongue twisters and things that are hard to say.

A selection of tongue twisters was written on posters and shown one after another—for individual volunteers or groups from the congregation to attempt. This led to the difficulty that we find in speaking praise or admitting fault, and the importance of taking the initiative in making peace with one's brother.

SONG
'They'll know we are Christians by our love'.

PRAYER of intercession
To the words: 'Lord, in your mercy' the congregation responds: 'Hear our prayer'

THE OFFERINGS
Brought forward to the Communion Table

PRAYER of dedication, said together:
O God our Father, with these our gifts we offer ourselves anew in your service. Take our lips and speak through them. Take our hands and work through

them. Take our hearts and set them on fire with love
for you and for our neighbours. We ask this for Jesus'
sake.   AMEN.

SONG
   'Go forth and tell'

THE BLESSING

(B) HEARING

WELCOME AND INTRODUCTION

SONG
   'Thank you'

VERSES FROM PSALM 19, said together:
   How clearly the sky reveals God's glory!
   How plainly it shows what he has done!
   Each day announces it to the following day;
   each night repeats it to the next.
   No speech or words are used, no sound is heard;
   yet their voice goes out to all the world
   and is heard to the ends of the earth.
   God made a home in the sky for the sun;
   it comes out in the morning like a happy bridegroom,
   like an athlete eager to run a race.
   It starts at one end of the sky
   and goes across to the other.

   May my words and my thoughts be acceptable to you,
   O Lord, my refuge and my redeemer!

PRAYER

SONG
   'Standing in the need of prayer'

BIBLE READING

ADDRESS: Sounds and things that are hard to hear.
Simon and Garfunkel's 'Sound of Silence' was played on record and 'The Sound of Music' on the organ. Then the congregation were invited to try to identify a variety of sounds which had been recorded—either from life or by transfer from a sound effects record—and which were played over the church stereo system. The theme was then developed with regard to different ways in which we can hear what God is saying—through his Word, through events, through the need of our neighbours.

PRAYER of intercession

SONG
'My Lord, what a morning'

THE OFFERINGS
Brought forward to the Communion Table.

PRAYER of dedication, said together:
Eternal God, we thank you for every experience through which you speak to us, and for Jesus Christ who is your living Word. Accept our gifts and speak to us of your mercy. Come into our world with your creative word, that your will may be done and your name glorified, forever.   AMEN.

HYMN 475
'We have heard a joyful sound'

THE BLESSING

(C) TASTING

WELCOME AND INTRODUCTION

SONG
'Praise and thanksgiving'

VERSES FROM PSALM 34, said together:
I will bless the Lord continually;
his praise shall be always on my lips.
O taste and see that the Lord is good;
Happy are those who find safety with him.
Obey the Lord, all his people;
those who obey him have all they need.
Even lions go hungry for lack of food,
but those who obey the Lord lack nothing good.
Come, my young friends, and listen to me,
and I will teach you to honour the Lord.
Would you like to enjoy life?
Do you want long life and happiness?
Then hold back from speaking evil and from telling
lies.
Turn away from evil and do good;
strive for peace with all your heart.

PRAYER

SONG
'Rejoice in the Lord'

BIBLE READING
Matthew 5:13-16.

ADDRESS: Testing taste and flavour.
Various opportunities were provided to try to identify
different tastes—potato crisps of different flavours,
bread spread with butter or margarine, 'real fruit'
pastilles, and several substances which looked like salt.
This led to a consideration of manna, the Passover, the
Lord's Supper, and being the salt of the world.

PRAYER of intercession

SONG
'My God loves me' *(Twentieth Century Folk Hymnal,
Vol. 1)*

THE OFFERINGS
Brought forward to the Communion Table.

PRAYER of dedication, said together:
Almighty God, you have called us to witness to the fulness of life in Jesus Christ. Accept our gifts and strengthen us by your Spirit. Let our light so shine before men, that they may see our good works and glorify our Father in heaven. We ask this in Jesus' name. AMEN.

SONG
'In the name of Jesus' (Tune: 'Camberwell', *Sound of Living Waters)*

THE BLESSING

9. A FAMILY COMMUNION SERVICE

At the beginning of the service, along with the Church Officer carrying the Bible, followed by the Minister, a family carried bread and wine to the Table.

HYMN

CALL TO PRAYER
   I know that your goodness and love will be with me all
   my life, and your house will be my home so long as I
   live (Ps. 23:6, TEV).

PRAYERS
   Let us praise God . . .

   God of power, God of love,
   God of here and now, God of every place and every
      day,
   God of us, God of all,
   We worship you, through Jesus Christ our Lord.

   We praise you
   that you have made this place your place,
   a home from home for us,
   where we may bring our happiness
   and turn it into praise for your goodness;

   where we may bring our questions
   and turn them into wonder at your greatness;
   where we may bring our troubles
   and turn them into trust in your loving care;

   where we may bring our sins and wrong,
   and turn them into new beginnings
   with your Spirit's help.

   Let us be quiet for a moment, and think what we bring
      to this place this day . . .

something to be thankful for . . .
something we are searching for . . .
something we are troubled about . . .
something we are ashamed of . . .

Let us bring it to God, and know his blessing,
and let us remember before God these words of long
ago,
and make them our prayer,

"I know that your goodness and love will be with me
all my life,
and your house will be my home as long as I live."

Thanks be to God!

SCRIPTURE READING
I Corinthians 11:23-26 (NEB, TEV, or Alan Dale
New World p. 291).

HYMN

BRIEF ADDRESS

OFFERING

PRAYERS
Here for our offerings, Lord God,
set down on this Table
alongside bread and wine;
sign of what you give us,
sign of what we can share.

For all we have, we give you thanks,

for the daily food and warmth and safety of home . . .
for the love and caring that surrounds us
whether we live with others or by ourselves . . .

for the Faith we share in the Church
and for the Bible that tells us
and for the hymns that sing it . . .

for Jesus who died for us
and lives for us
and brings us together to you ...

For all you give us, we give you thanks.

We pray for other people now,
for those who do not yet know their living Lord ...
for those who are unhappy, homeless, uncared for ...
for people passing through a time of sadness, illness,
   worry for the health and safety of someone dear to
   them ...
For them we pray, for we know we can trust you.

Our God and Father,
we are met now as a family
around your Table.

Give us your Spirit and bless this bread and wine, so
   that Jesus may fulfil his promise to us through them.

As we pass them from hand to hand,
turning to each other,
bring us close to Jesus,
and to each other in Jesus,

And as he taught his people, so we pray together 'Our
   Father ...'

HYMN
   *(During which elders come forward to stand before the
   Table.)*

INSTITUTION
   Here are God's gifts for God's people.

   In this we follow Jesus.

   On the side of a hill
   on the shore of a lake
   in the home of an outcast
   at the end of a journey
   Jesus in food and drink
   offered to his followers

fellowship with himself
and a foretaste of the new creation.

Most memorably of all
on the night of his arrest
HE TOOK BREAD
and said thanks to God
and BROKE IT
and shared it with his friends

Then HE TOOK THE CUP
and gave it to them.

"Do this", he said, "to remember me."

MINISTER'S COMMUNION

ELDERS' COMMUNION
(As each elder was served, he or she moved to serve the people.)

CONGREGATION'S COMMUNION

PRAYERS
Gracious God,
we say a blessing for a Father's gifts
and we go on our way
to live by them
at home and at work.

May we see in every family table
an image of the Communion Table.

May we see in all the daily good shared with others
the sign of your care.

May we carry into all our living
at home and with friends
something of the fellowship of the Church.

And unite us in the Spirit here and everywhere
with the rest of your family,
divided from us by distance or by death,
until the day of last homecoming to you and in you.

Through Jesus Christ our Lord
to whom be glory.

HYMN

BENEDICTION

*The Church Officer carries the Bible from the Church,
followed by the family with the bread and wine from the
Table, followed by the minister.*

NOTE: *Children and young people of 8-16 were present
with parents for this service. During preceding weeks there
had been preparation of both children and adults for it, and
the special arrangements at it carefully explained. Children
did not take bread and wine, but passed it along the pews as
the need arose.*

10. SERVICES PREPARED AND LED BY A CONGREGATIONAL GROUP ALONG WITH THE MINISTER

(A) ON THE THEME OF MONEY

CALL TO WORSHIP

SONG
'Praise and Thanksgiving' (a song on the theme of sharing the fruits of the earth, sung to the tune 'Bunessan', *New Church Praise*).

INTRODUCTION TO THE THEME
Playing of a track from Pink Floyd record on Money, which includes sound effects.

Brief discussion with neighbours on how they would spend a pools' win of half-a-million pounds. (This linked up with a current item of news. Talking with one's neighbour is the easiest form of discussion, though it is important to make the subject clear.)

Playing of track from 'Oliver' on Food.

Brief discussion on how much people eat in a self-service buffet. (A very few minutes are enough to allow immediate reaction, this time in open discussion.)

BIBLE READING
Luke 12:13-16.

DISCUSSION: Standard of Living.
(The contrast between the Bible passage and the earlier discussion provoked relevant comments.)

PRAYER
For forgiveness, and a sounder sense of stewardship.

SONG
> 'Sing Life, Sing Love, Sing Jesus' *(Twentieth Century Folk Hymnal, Vol. II)*—sung with guitar accompaniment.

THE OFFERINGS
> Brought forward to the Communion Table. Recorded music.

PRAYER of intercession, including special reference to those in need.
> (One member of the group composed this prayer.)

SONG
> 'Go forth and tell' *(Sound of Living Waters)*

THE BLESSING

(B) ON THE THEME OF NEWS

ORGAN VOLUNTARY

RECORDED NEWS BULLETIN
> (The service began with the playing of the 9 a.m. news of that day. It was a very effective way of earthing the service in the real situation).

CALL TO WORSHIP

PRAYER

INTRODUCTION—on the theme News.

SONG
> 'This is the day' *(Sound of Living Waters)*

TALKING WITH NEIGHBOURS
> The best news you have ever had . . .(People contribute their own experience).

REPORTING AND DISCUSSION
> Why do newspapers not print good news?

Do people hear so much news that they hardly notice what it is about?—e.g. violence and bloodshed.

Can news do harm?—e.g. publicity for hooliganism.

What difference does it make to us that we can hear news from anywhere in the world?

Playing of track from Simon and Garfunkel—Silent Night/9 o'clock news.

SHORT COMMENT

Christianity is about Good News.

The Good News Bible has sold one million copies.

We have good news to share.
(Though such a service starts from experience, it normally moves on to a positive Christian statement—a form of proclamation.)

SONG

'Go, tell everyone' (in *Twentieth Century Folk Hymnal*, Vol. I. A paraphrase of the opening verses of Luke 4.)

THE OFFERINGS

Brought forward to the Communion Table.
(Recorded music: 'If I had a hammer'—by Peter, Paul and Mary.)

BIBLE READING

Mark 1:1, 2, 4, 14, 15.
(Here the Bible reading came last, but in the context its significance was heightened.)

PRAYER

With special reference to the church's task of proclamation.

SONG

'Go forth and tell' *(Sound of Living Waters)*

THE BLESSING

(C)   ON THE THEME OF POLLUTION

ORGAN VOLUNTARY

CALL TO WORSHIP

HYMN 154
'All things bright and beautiful'

PRAYER

THE OFFERINGS
Brought forward to the Communion Table.

Recorded music: 'Remember you're a Womble'.

(The simple movement of walking forward is a regular part of the service. On this occasion a number of crisp packets were left in passages and under pews.)

INTRODUCTION—on the theme Pollution.
Newspaper reading (a current example of an oil tanker accident).

Thoughts on the theme—statistics read over recorded music by Joan Baez ('What have they done to the rain?'). The statistics referred to atmospheric pollution in America and other examples from different parts of the world.

Discussion. In general discussion there was inevitably a plea that 'something should be done'.

EXAMPLES of local pollution.
Reactions . . .

(The crisp papers were collected and a box produced with rubbish gathered from the church grounds before the service. Local examples of rubbish dumping were mentioned; and the discussion moved to the question of whether people were prepared to do anything in their own community.)

SINGING
   'Our Father' (a version of the Lord's Prayer with music
   by Estelle White). Guitar accompaniment.

BIBLE READING
   Verses from Psalm 24, beginning 'The earth is the
   Lord's'.

   Brief comment by the minister.

PRAYER
   Composed by a member of the group.

SONG
   'Morning has broken'

THE BLESSING

(D) ON THE THEME OF HEALTH

ORGAN VOLUNTARY

CALL TO WORSHIP

RECORDED MUSIC
   'The Rivers of Babylon' (Boney M)

PRAYER
   (A prayer of approach, incorporating the words of the
   Psalm from the record.)

SONG
   'Light up the fire' (sung with guitar accompaniment).
   (Twentieth Century Folk Hymnal, Vol. II.)

THEME: Keeping Fit
   Recorded Interviews (jogging and yoga)
       (Two local enthusiasts had been inter-
       viewed—one committed to early morning jog-
       ging, the other a keen member of a yoga class.

They were asked why they took part in these activities, and what they thought the benefits were. The jogger replied: 'I'm running for my life.'

The use of interviews helps to relate the worship in church to the outside world. They are played through the sound system so that they are clearly heard.)

Discussion

(People were quick to react. Though discussion can't be planned, it naturally led to a point where someone asked if fitness were only physical or if it had to do with the whole personality.)

THE OFFERINGS

Brought forward to the Communion Table. (During which organ music was played.)

BIBLE READING and comment on 'Fulness of life'.

PRAYER of intercession

SONG

'Sing Life, Sing Love, Sing Jesus'

THE BLESSING

B. SERVICES FOR SEASONS OF THE CHRISTIAN YEAR

1. AN ADVENT CANDLE CEREMONY

A different family of father, mother and young person may be invited to take part in this ceremony on each Sunday during Advent. It is probably best to incorporate the ceremony at an early point in the service.

Four red candles and one larger white candle are used. A holder may easily be made of wood or metal to accommodate these, with the white Christmas candle standing at the centre of a circle, or behind a row, formed by the four red Advent candles.

Advent I

Voice 1 (Young person)   Voice 2 (Mother)
Voice 3 (Father)

Voice 1: One candle to remind us of the Advent hope in which all ages have looked forward to the coming of the Lord.

Voice 2: "In the days after that time of trouble, the sun will grow dark, the moon will no longer shine, the stars will fall from heaven, and the powers in space will be driven from their courses. Then the Son of Man will appear, coming in the clouds with great power and glory. He will send the angels out to the four corners of the earth to gather God's chosen people from one end of the earth to the other."

Voice 3: Lord Jesus, we thank you for your promise to return to this world, not as a tiny baby but as a triumphant king. Keep us watchful against temptation, and joyous in your service, for your name's sake.   AMEN.

81

As the first red candle is lit, the congregation sings verses 1 and 2 of the song. (See words on page 84.)

Advent II
(the first candle being already lit)

VOICE 1:   The second candle, to remind us of God's gift of the Bible, which bears witness to our Lord.

VOICE 2:   "So we are even more confident of the message proclaimed by the prophets. You will do well to pay attention to it, because it is like a lamp shining in a dark place until the Day dawns and the light of the morning star shines in your hearts."

VOICE 3:   Heavenly Father, you have shown the wonder of your love for us in Jesus Christ through the Bible. Grant that in the written Word, and through the spoken Word, we may behold the living Word, our Saviour Jesus Christ.   AMEN.

The second red candle is lit as verses 1-3 of the song are sung.

Advent III
(the first two candles being already lit)

VOICE 1:   The third candle, to remind us of John the Baptist and all God's messengers who prepare the way for the Saviour's coming.

VOICE 2:   "The light shines on in the darkness and the darkness has not overcome it. There was a man sent from God whose name was John. He came to bear witness to the light, that all might believe through him."

VOICE 3:   Almighty God, give your people grace to enter on the way of salvation. As they listen to the voice of John, the Lord's herald, bring them safely to Jesus whom John foretold.   AMEN.

The third candle is lit as verses 1-4 are sung.

Advent IV
(three candles already lit)

VOICE 1: The fourth candle, to remind us of Mary who humbly received God's will as her own.

VOICE 2: "And Mary said 'Behold the handmaid of the Lord; be it unto me according to thy word'."

VOICE 3: O God our Father, we thank you for the joyful experience of Mary. Help us to honour her lowly grace and to share in the humility which does not despise the Christ who comes as a child born in a stable.

The fourth candle is lit as verses 1-5 are sung.

Christmas Eve

The four red candles should be lit before the service begins. At midnight the white candle is lit, with Scripture sentences and prayer such as the following:

'Unto us a child is born; unto us a son is given. Glory to God in the highest, and on earth peace, goodwill toward men.'

O God our Father, as we remember the birth of your son Jesus Christ, we welcome him with gladness as Saviour, and pray that there may always be room for him in our hearts and in our homes, for his sake.   AMEN.

As the white candle is lit the congregation sings the complete song.

The white candle may be lit for services during the Christmas season (e.g. until the second Sunday after Christmas).

The Song
(Tune: 'The Holly and the Ivy')

1. The holly and the ivy
   Are dancing in a ring
   Round the berry-bright red candles
   And the white and shining King.

2. And ONE is for God's people
   In every age and day
   We are watching for His coming
   We believe and we obey.

3. And TWO is for the prophets
   And for the light they bring
   They are candles in the darkness
   All alight for Christ the King.

4. And THREE for John the Baptist
   He calls on us to sing
   O prepare the way for Jesus Christ
   He is coming, Christ the King.

5. And FOUR for Mother Mary
   "I cannot see the Way
   But you promise me a baby
   I believe you—I obey."

6. And Christ is in the centre
   For this is His Birthday
   With the shining lights of Christmas
   Singing "He has come to-day".

2.   A CHRISTMAS SERVICE

The service summarised below was used at a Gift Service on the Fourth Sunday in Advent. Over a hundred children from the Junior Department of the Sunday School were involved, either miming or singing. In a large building with fixed pews, possibilities for movement are limited—but the use of lights can help to focus attention on different parts of the building. The sermon was divided into small units of two or three minutes each, and the congregation was provided with orders of service. Such services require considerable time and rehearsal—but the effort is perhaps more rewarding than when devoted to a traditional Children's Nativity Play, since the whole congregation is involved.

PRAYER of Invocation

CALL TO WORSHIP

HYMN 165
'O come, O come, Immanuel'

I   THE WORLD'S NEED

SERMON (i)
The pervasive effect of the Fall of Man—dividing people from each other and from God.

While the minister spoke, children moved into the church representing the effects of sin and evil in the world—e.g. Idolatry (groups carrying idols and horoscopes); Greed (workers carrying placards with slogans); Oppression (slaves); Suffering (a hungry Indian family); Loneliness and Neurosis (individuals with bottles of pills and whisky bottles). The lights were out in the main part of the church, and the children moved back into the darkness, taking up a position in the aisles.

JUNIOR CHOIR (in back gallery)
'God who created this Eden of earth, What have we done?' *(Songs for the Seventies)*

PRAYERS of Confession and Supplication

II THE WORLD'S RESCUE

SERMON (ii)
The beginning of God's redemptive work, and his preparation of Israel (Abraham . . . Moses . . . Isaiah). The prophets' longing for God's deliverance, and God's answer to that longing.

Reading: St. John 1 : 1-5, 10-14. (Spotlight on manger in chancel).

CHURCH CHOIR
'Ding Dong, merrily on high'

CONGREGATION: HYMN 176
'Still the Night'

SERMON (iii)
Incorporating Matthew's account of the Wise Men (again with enactment by Junior children). The symbolism of their gifts—and the symbolism of our Christmas presents.

CONGREGATION: HYMN 191
'O come, all ye faithful'
(During which the Primary and Beginners children entered church with their gifts.)

III THE COMING FULFILMENT

SERMON (iv)
A look forward from Bethlehem to the work of Christ with, at the end, a Cross of light projected on to the

back wall, behind the manger. (The children who had previously brought symbols of the evil in the world now moved forward slowly towards the chancel.)

JUNIOR CHOIR
'Christ is the Lord of the Smallest Atom' *(Youth Praise,* Vol. II)

PRAYER of Intercession

CONGREGATION: HYMN 194
'Love came down at Christmas'

THE SACRAMENT OF BAPTISM
The incorporation of another member into the new humanity.

SERMON (v)
The continuing struggle against evil, and our hope of the world's fulfilment, made possible because of Bethlehem and Calvary.

CHURCH CHOIR
'Hallelujah! For the Lord God omnipotent reigneth'

THE OFFERINGS

PRAYER of Dedication

HYMN 169
'Hark! The Herald Angels sing'

BENEDICTION

3. A FORM OF SERVICE FOR EACH DAY OF HOLY WEEK

INTRODUCTORY SENTENCES

HYMN

PRAYER—said responsively:

MINISTER: You are the one and only God;
There is none like you, Lord;
You are great and your name is holy.

PEOPLE: With what shall we come before the Lord,
the God of heaven, when we come to worship him?

MINISTER: The Lord has told us what is good.
What he requires of us is this:
To do what is just, to show constant love,
And to live in humble fellowhip with our God.

Let us confess our sins to Almighty God.

Silence

PEOPLE: Most merciful God,
We confess that we have sinned in thought, word and deed.
We have not loved you with our whole heart.
We have not loved our neighbours as ourselves.
In your mercy, forgive what we have been,
help us to amend what we are,
and direct what we shall be,
through Jesus Christ our Lord.

MINISTER: Christ Jesus came into the world to save sinners.

Hear then the word of grace and the assurance of pardon:
Your sins are forgiven for his sake.

PEOPLE: Almighty God, your Son Jesus Christ has gone before us in the way of total trust and obedience to you.
Humble us by his example. By the working of your Holy Spirit, inspire us to follow in his way, that we may share in the power of his Resurrection.

These prayers we offer in Jesus' name.   AMEN.

SCRIPTURE READING
The record of the day.

SONG
1. Were you there when they crucified my Lord?
    Were you there when they crucified my Lord?
    Oh—sometimes it causes me to tremble, tremble, tremble
    Were you there when they crucified my Lord?

2. *(Mon.)* Were you there when he cleansed the temple court?
    (Tue.) Were you there when he taught the truth of God?
    (Wed.) Were you there when he spoke of costly love?
    (Thu.) Were you there when he shared the bread and wine?
    (Fri.) Were you there when they pierced him in the side?

3. Were you there when they nailed him to a tree? . . .

4. Were you there when he rose from out the tomb?

SERMON

*OFFERING brought forward

PRAYER of Thanksgiving and Intercession

HYMN

BENEDICTION

*(*From this point on the Thursday, the service runs as follows:*

CONFESSION OF FAITH

OFFERING brought forward

PRAYER of Intercession

BENEDICTION

HYMN

SACRAMENT OF HOLY COMMUNION)

4. WORD AND EUCHARIST FOR HOLY WEEK (PALM SUNDAY)

This service was led by ten teenagers, six girls and four boys. It was decided to have seven units in which the events of Holy Week might be experienced. Each unit was devised separately. We considered how all five senses might be involved, and this was achieved. New songs and music were composed for the service.

1. ENTRY INTO JERUSALEM
    Luke 19:35-38 was read, and the group entered from the rear of the Church, singing 'Welcome King' to a fast rhythm. Scarves were waved, daffodils given out to people in the pews, and 'Jesus stickers' placed on lapels; thus the pews were invaded, and contact made with everyone—more happy than violent. Flashing disco lights were used. Before settling down, the group sang 'Disciples' Song' while walking round the Communion Table (with a pause for the reading of Luke 20:41-42).

2. THE NEW TEMPLE
    After the tumultuous entry, it was felt that people might think again about the Cleansing of the Temple if it was done very quietly, with the emphasis on the provision of a new way to God in Christ.

    Luke 19:45-46 was read.

    Dialogue between boy (scribe) and girl (would-be-worshipper) around a cash register had contemporary note—what we are asked to 'do' before we can see God. Eventually, girl turns away towards sound of singing—'I am the Way—You can't get to God but by me'.

3. DEBATE WITH THE JEWS
    Mark 11:27-33; 12:13-27.

    This was comic relief. Scribes, Pharisees and Sadd-
    uccees raised their issues to background of 'The Old
    Sanhedrin had a Committee' (tune: *Old Macdonald*).
    The straight replies to the music-hall-sounding ques-
    tions came from the *pews,* as there was no attempt to
    act or portray the figure of our Lord.

4. WEDNESDAY
    Matthew 26:6-13. After a time of silence, hymn 428
    was sung unaccompanied as an act of adoration.

5. GETHSEMANE
    Mark 14:27-36.

    Lights dimmed. The sound of a metronome ticking
    (imminence of betrayal). A song from the side 'Thy
    Will be Done'. After the verses, while the tune was
    hummed, a boy led prayer for forgiveness of our
    weakness, and of praise for our Lord's obedience to
    the Father.

    The disciples scatter.

6. TRIAL
    This was starkly portrayed, simply by reading alter-
    nately from the Gospel accounts and passages from
    contemporary accounts of persecution (Wurmbrand,
    Vins etc.).

7. CALVARY
    John 19:17-19.

    Sound from vestibule of nails being driven home. A
    large rough cross was carried in and held in spotlights.
    Roman nails and crown of thorns passed from person
    to person in the pews.

Song: 'What man is this?'—from L.P. 'I've never known a love like this' by Chico Holiday (Pilgrim King).

The Words from the Cross were then repeated from different locations, by a boy who moved about in the darkened Church. All lights were extinguished for several minutes, during which a thurible of incense was taken round the church (the rest in the Tomb) and the Holy Table was being laid with white linen. *(Doing all this in darkness had been practised.)* The sound of stone grinding on stone . . .

8. RESURRECTION

The Orthodox greeting—'Christ is risen: He is risen indeed'—builds up, and the lights all go on for the first time. 'The Angel rolled the Stone away' *(Faith, Folk and Clarity)* sung as a processional during the entry of the Communion elements. The Order used was the third order from *The Divine Service*. The Kyrie, the Creed, Sanctus, Benedictus qui venit, Lord's Prayer, Agnus Dei and final Amen were all sung to new music. Two ministers took part with one chalice and one paten. The congregation received Communion kneeling before the Table, and in most cases were addressed by name and blessed. 'Disciples' Song' used as recessional. The service lasted 1½-2 hours, and was attended by a congregation of around 200.

'Welcome King', 'Disciples' Song', 'Thy Will be Done', 'I am the Way', were all composed locally for the occasion.

5. A SERVICE FOR EASTER DAY

OPENING ACCLAMATION
MINISTER: The Lord is risen
CONGREGATION: He is risen indeed.

HYMN 264
'Jesus Christ is risen today'

PRAYER

THE EASTER STORY, for children
(Told in verse, with pictures).

HYMN 282
'Come, ye children'

LESSON
Mark 16:1-7.

SERMON
(A family service is for adults as well as children and, particularly at Easter, it was important to include a short sermon.)

OFFERING
Brought forward for Dedication.

PRAYER of Dedication and Intercession:
TO THE WORDS: For these we would pray
THE RESPONSE IS: Lord, hear our prayer
                      (A simple response is a basic form of participation.)

SONG
'He is risen, tell the story' *(Twentieth Century Folk Hymnal,* Vol. III)

SACRAMENT OF HOLY COMMUNION

PRAYER of Thanksgiving—Response

MINISTER: Lift up your hearts

CONGREGATION: We lift them to the Lord

MINISTER: Let us give thanks to the Lord our God

CONGREGATION: It is right to give him thanks and praise.

CONCLUDING PRAYER—Response

MINISTER: Let us praise the Lord

CONGREGATION: Christ has died
                 Christ is risen
                 In Christ shall all be made alive.
                 Blessing and honour and glory and power be to our God for ever and ever.

(It was important that children sitting with their families should follow the Communion. A simple leaflet was provided for them with drawings and explanation. The wording was also kept brief and simple—along lines suggested in the Partners in Learning *service.)*

SONG

'Lord of the dance'
(During the singing the whole congregation moved to the Church Hall where a full breakfast—with boiled eggs—had been prepared. Having taken part in the Sacrament, the congregation, including children, shared a common meal. There was an atmosphere of celebration and also of continuing worship.)

BREAKFAST

shared together

SONGS

'Alleluia, alleluia, give thanks to the risen Lord'
'Light up the fire'

(Led by group with guitars. There was at this stage a resumption—though in an informal setting—of the worship.)

DREAMS OF CELEBRATION
(From *Interrobang!* by Norman Habel. A splendid visionary litany for two voices; in this case said by Minister and the whole congregation.)

SONG
'Jesus Christ is alive today' (From *Sound of Living Waters)*

BENEDICTION

6. A SERVICE FOR PENTECOST

This service, in the progression of its three sections, is an attempt to recover the experience of Pentecost for the congregation.

In preparing the church, posters based on the Pentecostal symbols of wind and fire may be displayed. 'Cut-outs' suggesting tongues of flame may be fixed in place against windows.

As the service begins, some children are lighting candles placed in the chancel and/or round the church. The minister on entering is handed a taper by one of the children and joins in briefly before turning to the congregation.

MINISTER: To-day is Pentecost, the birthday of the Church!

'Flesh can give birth only to flesh; it is spirit that gives birth to spirit.

You ought not to be astonished, then, when I tell you that you must be born over again.

The wind blows where it wills; you hear the sound of it, but you do not know where it comes from, or where it is going.

So with everyone who is born from spirit.'

(John 3:6-8)

HYMN 46
'This is the day of light'

PRAYER
A collect or similar short prayer, on the theme of 'light' or 'new birth', for example:

"Almighty God, we give you thanks
   for this life and all its blessings,
   for joys great and simple,
   for gifts and powers more than we deserve,
   for love at the heart of your purpose
   and a surpassing wisdom in all your works,
   for light in the world
   brought once in Christ and shining ever
      through his Spirit.
We pray, through Jesus Christ our Lord,
   for that light to dawn upon us daily,
   that we may always have a grateful heart,
   and a will to love and to serve
   to the end of our days.
Lord, hear our prayer and our praises:
Alleluia, we bless you, O God."

(The Daily Office, p. 129)

Waiting for the Spirit

Minister's introduction along these lines:

Birthdays are not only a beginning but an outcome, the outcome of meeting, marrying, loving and caring . . .Similarly, the birthday of the Church was preceded by the loving activity of God in Christ, his life, death and rising again . . .The Book of Acts, the book of the Holy Spirit, begins with the Resurrection . . .

HYMN of the Resurrection

The minister introduces the 'Prayers of waiting' on the following lines:

The disciples wait; the continuation of their tasks, in resignation or in expectancy: their life together in the breaking of bread—and in prayer . . .

THE PRAYERS

A series of meditative prayers, with silences, including confession.

The Experience of the Spirit

After due pause, at a given signal one of the following acclamations is made by several voices in several languages successively:

Christ has died.
Christ is risen.
In Christ shall all be made alive.
Blessing and honour and glory and power be to our God for ever and ever.

Christ is Victor.
Christ is King.
Christ is Lord of all.

Praise the Lord!
Dying you destroyed our death.
Rising you restored our life.
Lord Jesus, come in glory.

Praise be to the God and Father of our Lord Jesus Christ.
In his mercy he gives us new birth into a living hope by the resurrection of Jesus Christ from the dead.

(All the above from *The Daily Office,* p. 130f.)

Come Lord Jesus, Lord Jesus come.

Raise us up from fear, Lord of the Living!
Raise us up from fear, Lord of the Living!

(These and other similar acclamations are from *Risk,* Vol. II, No. 2-3, 1975—the Nairobi worship book—and are offered in three languages.)

The doors of the church may then be opened and appropriate music played (on record or by organist). The music fades as a succession of speakers in turn stand in their places throughout the congregation and declaim each a sentence of the following:

"All who are moved by the Spirit are sons of God.

The Spirit aids our weakness, pleading for God's own
people in God's own way.

Our sufferings are as nothing to the freedom of God's
children.

Nothing can separate us from God's love, in Jesus
Christ our Lord.

The victory is ours.

The Spirit sets us free."

(The Daily Office, p. 131)

MINISTER: "Here is the proof that we dwell in him and
he dwells in us: he has imparted his Spirit
to us."

(I John 14:13)

HYMN
'Hail thee Festival Day' (CH 3. 328) or other Pentecost hymn.

Working with the Spirit

GOSPEL READING
Matthew 16:24-28.

SERMON
on 'Launching Out' based on gospel reading.

HYMN
'O breath of life' (CH 3. 339)

'Holy Spirit ever living' (CH 3. 334)

'Go tell everyone' *(Sounds of Living Waters,* No. 93)

'Sing, one and all, a song of celebration' *(New Church
Praise,* 87)

'There's a spirit in the air' *(New Church Praise,* 98)

OFFERING
During which 'Bird of Heaven' (Sydney Carter) may
be sung as solo *(Faith, Folk and Festivity).*

Thereafter, the congregation will together make an affirmation, such as:

MINISTER: Let us affirm our desire to grow up by increasing harmony among all peoples, all races together, rich and poor together, young and old together.

ALL: Yes, Lord, so says my heart.

MINISTER: Let us affirm our desire to grow up working together, for justice and peace in all the world.

ALL: Yes, Lord, so says my heart.

MINISTER: Let us affirm our desire to grow up in caring for the weak, the unprotected, the sick, the hungry, those who are in prison.

ALL: Yes, Lord, so says my heart.

MINISTER: Let us affirm our desire to grow up in responsibility for citizenship, for guaranteeing human rights.

ALL: Yes, Lord, so says my heart.

MINISTER: Let us affirm our desire to grow up in love and respect for members of our family, for the neighbours with whom we live, for the persons with whom we work, for the members of Christ's Church.

ALL: Yes, Lord, so says my heart.

(Drafted by a group of African women in 1969: in *Worship and Wonder,* p. 61.)

Further prayers and/or the Lord's Prayer may be added.

(Other affirmations are found in *Risk*—see above.)

HYMN

From the list above.

DISMISSAL AND BENEDICTION

"Go now: you are God's people.

Find your strength in his mighty power.

Take up his armour,

so that you may stand your ground when things are at
their worst;

complete every task,

and still stand.

And the blessing of God,

Father, Son and Holy Spirit,

go with you all."

(Prayers for Contemporary Worship, p. 91)

7. AN INTERCESSION FOR ALL SAINTS DAY

MINISTER: In our prayers for others on this (Sunday after) All Saints' Day, we remember especially all who belong with us to the whole family of God's people.

VOICE 1: Who are the saints?

VOICES 2, 3: We are the saints.

VOICE 1: All of us?

VOICES 2, 3: Yes, all of us!

VOICE 1: The living, too?

VOICES 2, 3: The living and the dead: one family in heaven and on earth.

VOICE 1: What makes us saints?

VOICE 2: Our Baptism

VOICE 3: Our belonging in the Church

VOICE 2: Our faith in Christ.

VOICE 1: And our goodness too?

VOICES 2, 3: God's goodness, not ours!

VOICE 2: All saints are forgiven sinners.

VOICE 3: Forgiven sinners are all saints.

VOICE 1: Saints and sinners:

VOICE 2: Sinners and saints.

VOICE 3: Love and forgiveness:

VOICE 1: Forgiveness and love.

VOICE 2: Heaven and earth:

VOICE 3: Earth and heaven.

VOICE 1:   Past and present:
VOICE 2:   Present and past.

MINISTER: Let us pray
VOICE 1:   With Peter
VOICES 2, 3: Give us faith like a rock
VOICE 1:   With Andrew
VOICES 2, 3: Help us to bring men to Christ
VOICE 1:   With John the Baptist
VOICES 2, 3: Show us your kingdom in the affairs of men.
VOICE 1:   With Mary Magdalene
VOICES 2, 3: Give us a flair for gracious deeds.
VOICE 1:   With John the Beloved Disciple
VOICES 2, 3: Bring us to love our Master.
VOICE 1:   With Thomas
VOICES 2, 3: Grant that we may cry, "My Lord and my
              God!"

MINISTER: Now let us pray for those who make up the
              communion of saints.
VOICE 1:   Let us pray for all baptized Christians (espe-
              cially for the little child to be baptized here).

MINISTER: Lord, hear us.
PEOPLE: Lord, graciously hear us.
VOICE 2:   Let us pray for all who belong to the church
              of Christ, especially for all our fellow-
              Christians in this congregation.

MINISTER: Lord, hear us.
PEOPLE: Lord, graciously hear us.

VOICE 3: Let us pray for all whose faith in Christ is growing and maturing, that they may see its meaning for their lives.

MINISTER: Lord, hear us.

PEOPLE: Lord, graciously hear us.

VOICE 1: And let us give thanks for all Christians of other ages and of other lands who, with us, make up the communion of saints.

MINISTER: Glory be to the Father, and to the Son, and to the Holy Spirit:

PEOPLE: As it was in the beginning, is now, and ever shall be, world without end.

ALL: AMEN.

C. WORSHIP ON OTHER OCCASIONS

1. A 'TALENTS EVENING'

A Service of Worship for the Woman's Guild

The Leader points out that there are two dictionary meanings of talent. The first is "an ancient unit of weight or of money". This is symbolised by the offering and dedication of special envelopes. The second meaning is "any natural or special gift: a special aptitude or ability". These are demonstrated by members of the branch in the following ways (or otherwise as appropriate):

Singing (and accompanying)

Recitation

Dancing (perhaps a reel which has involved also the talent of a member in teaching dancing)

Writing (a poem by a Guild member)

Drawing or painting

Floral art.

This can lead on to the consideration of household chores—dishes, cleaning, ironing—as the offering of talents (with readings from Marjorie Holmes—I've got to talk to Somebody, God).

HYMN

(Tune: *Camberwell*)

1. When in his own image
    God created man,
    He included freedom
    In creation's plan.
    For he loved us even
    From before our birth:
    By his grace he made us
    Freemen of this earth.

2.   God to man entrusted
     Life as gift and aim.
     Sin became our prison
     Turning hope to shame.
     Man against his brother
     Lifted hand and sword:
     And the Father's pleading
     Went unseen, unheard.

3.   Then in time our maker
     Chose to intervene,
     Set his love in person
     In the human scene.
     Jesus broke the circle
     Of repeated sin
     So that man's devotion
     Newly might begin.

4.   Choose we now in freedom
     Where we should belong;
     Let us turn to Jesus,
     Let our choice be strong.
     May the great obedience
     Which in Christ we see
     Perfect all our service;
     Then we shall be free.

(The words may be interpreted through mime or movement.)

PRAYER

Dear Father, whether we possess one talent or many talents, bless us all, for we are your children—striving to understand the complexities of this life. Let your healing and cleansing love flow over us now . . . We ask it all in Jesus' name.   AMEN.

2. A MARRIED COUPLES' SERVICE

The service was designed to focus attention on the Christian concepts of love and marriage, to give thanks for the blessings of married life and to give married couples an opportunity to renew their vows together in church and show their appreciation of one another. Two hundred couples married in the five years of the current ministry were traced and invited. Where distance was too great, a couple was asked to attend their local church and join silently in prayer with and for all the other couples. This was a normal Sunday morning service, and it was made clear that unmarried people were not excluded, taking the opportunity to give thanks for the love of their parents and for the happy homes in which they had been brought up. Likewise, widows and widowers could give thanks for the years of happiness they had known with their partners, and perhaps pray God's blessing on the marriages of their own sons and daughters. Orders of service were duplicated on folding service sheets.

CALL TO WORSHIP

HYMN 72
    'O God of Bethel' or 360 'Praise my soul'

PRAYER

HYMN

READINGS as in marriage service.

HYMN 523
    'O happy home' (tune: 'O perfect love')

SERMON

OFFERING

PRAYER—Responsive
    The congregation standing, couples joining hands.

MINISTER: God our Father
we your children praise you
as we praised you on our wedding day
for your sacred gift of love
and for the institution of marriage.

PEOPLE: We bless you
for all the joy you have granted us together
over the years
and likewise for your grace
that has enabled us to surmount together
life's trials and sorrows.

MINISTER: In your presence we recall now
the sacred vows we made.

PEOPLE: We remember that we took each other
to have and to hold
from that day forward
for better or for worse
for richer or for poorer
in sickness and in health
to love and to cherish
till death should us part.

MINISTER: We remember that we made these promises
not only to each other
but to you.

PEOPLE: And solemnly now in your sight
we resolve afresh
that we shall be to each other
loving, faithful and dutiful husbands and
wives
as long as we shall live.
So help us God.

MINISTER: By the holy example of Jesus
Who loved us all with an unchanging love
and unwearying patience

PEOPLE: O help us God.

MINISTER: By the power of your Holy Spirit
           who is able to strengthen us and guide us

PEOPLE: O help us God.

MINISTER: Confirm the faith we have
           that undying love and loyalty
           are your will for us

PEOPLE: And so make our homes happy,
           our community healthy,
           and our nation strong,
           and bring nearer the day
           of your perfect Kingdom.

MINISTER: Through Jesus Christ our Lord

PEOPLE: AMEN.

HYMN 524
'Thy Kingdom come, yea bid it come'

BENEDICTION

3. INFORMAL WORSHIP FOR A SMALL GROUP

'Let's Play a Game'

First used to round off a season's meeting of house groups, whose topics had included the National Health Service, Devolution, Nuclear Energy, the Holy Spirit, Worship.

'I piped for you and you would not dance: I wept and wailed but you would not mourn.'

Jesus finds in the play of children illuminating commentary on the manners of the adult world.

SONG

'Let's play a game' (Malcolm Stewart, *Jesus Folk)*

(One verse runs:

I set a riddle to the rulers of the land:
Is your God's law dearer than a man's right hand?
Would you be sons of God or sons of Man?
And don't you hear the children for they understand?

and one chorus is:

Let's play a game
Let's pretend that love is each man's name
Let's see if the world remains the same.)

'All work and no play makes Jack a dull boy'—and the church a dull place. But do we usually get those the wrong way round? Do we think of worship as 'the serious side'—the work, while the rest is more like play, less solemn at any rate—Guilds, clubs, groups.

But is it not worship that should be more like play, when we rejoice, celebrate, imagine the world as it could be. When children play, they are working their way into life, preparing for the future. When we worship, we're working our way into the new people Jesus invites us to be and acting out the future he promises for us and all people.

111

So how will we play? What are the rules as we take this half-hour to relax together and reflect on our work in groups and celebrate our discoveries over the weeks we met?

Let's gather our thoughts, like in a prayer, as we recall what we talked about. Let's close our eyes ...Think about the night we discussed each topic now to be mentioned, where we met, whose house we were in, who was there, anything said that struck home ...Let us, with eyes closed, let things come back to us ...

Health ...the NHS, the danger that people are swallowed up in an impersonal system, and the great need to let people *participate* in their own cure, contribute to it, perhaps by altering their style of life or even their beliefs ...

(Pause)

Scottish Government ...and the need to bring people and decision-makers closer together so that we can *participate* in making the policies that govern our lives ...

(Pause)

Nuclear energy ...and why we must not only ask what our country needs, but add—what are other peoples' needs, so that we share in *(participate* in) their problems, even at the expense of our own careful programming.

(Pause)

The Holy Spirit ...letting the Spirit move freely in our world, letting it take its place, play a part, being open to it, *participating* with it.

(Pause)

Worship ...and the great cry that the people should be enabled to take more part, *participate* more, not leaving all to one person.

That's what we are going to do now—participate in worship, and further than worship. Let's play a game! Let's pretend that participating, sharing, is possible—with each other and in the world. Will you open your eyes?

The first game
is a singing game

Sharing doesn't mean everybody learns to do the same thing or become the same. It means bringing what is special that you have and being ready to accept what someone else has. Here is a really enjoyable Christian song which does just that—a song in which you and I have different parts and both are needed to keep things going.

SONG
'It's the Lord who comes' (in *Leap my soul)*

Other verses added for occasion:
To share in our life
To sit where we sit
To work where we work
To laugh when we laugh
To weep in our grief.

Let's play our second game

Let us stay relaxed by keeping the atmosphere of worship. Behind your seats is a sheet of paper (secured by Bluetack). Use it to identify yourself, without giving your name: 'I am a...', 'I am specially interested in...', 'Often I worry that...' are examples of how to begin. Put the paper back where you found it.

Now move round four places (try not to identify whose place you are going to). Take the paper and read it. Think your way into that person's shoes, 'under their skins'. End with a silent prayer for them...(they comply).

A plate will now come round: put the papers in it, offering your concern for another person to God. We have carried the burden of one person, he carries the burdens of every living person. As the plate goes round, a well-known song will start up in which you are asked to join in at least the last two lines of each verse which act as a chorus.

SONG
    'When I needed a neighbour' (Carter)

Plate, bread and wine are laid on the table, if not there already.

Now for our last game

We have pretended we are someone else: we have *become* that person for a minute or two and we may not quickly forget what it is like to be that person, to be in other people's shoes.

In the last game, our 'let's pretend' becomes for real, when Jesus steps into our shoes, when we are *in* him and *with* each other, playing out the great feast when all will gather round his table in love in a world transformed.

The bread will be unwrapped, for it is subject to no programme or policy of man's devising; the wine will be poured out, for it stands for a love which is too great to be contained or patterned by any human wit or ingenuity.

After the prayer and after each person has received both bread and wine, let each one join his voice in the singing of 'Peace will come', so that when we all have shared in the Lord we are every one of us singing 'Peace', both for ourselves and for all who do not yet participate in the peace we know.

But first, hear the Gospel.

'By this time they had reached the village to which they were going . . .he took bread and said the blessing . . ."Did we not feel our hearts on fire as he talked with us on the road and explained the scriptures to us?"' (Luke 24:28-32).

We too share such a meal, a meal which reaches deep into the past and brings fresh to our minds the meals over which Jesus and his disciples faced each other, challenging, loving, saving:

a meal which reaches deep into the present day, symbol of a unity and a sharing in a world of torn relationships and broken hopes:

a meal which reaches forward, offering a foretaste of the future when all will be round the table of the Lord.

Let us pray. 'Lord, bread can be a symbol of greed, wine the symbol of deep loneliness. Make them for us symbols of a sharing and a love which cannot be contained in any vessel of man's making or in any system, or in any church.   AMEN.'

'Let's play a game
Let's pretend that love is each man's name
Let's see if the world remains the same.'

Share this . . . and this . . .

SONG
        'Peace will come' (Paxton)

'It is finished: the game is ended: go forth and worship the Lord in all you think and say and do—tonight, tomorrow and for ever.'

4. A CHRISTIAN AID SERVICE

A Diet of Worship for Christian Aid

NOTE: *This outline is based on the duplicated order which is provided for Family Services. Brief explanations have been added in brackets.*

CALL TO WORSHIP

HYMN 367
'For the beauty of the earth'

SETTING THE TABLE
(A meal was demonstrated, though without actual cooking. A table was brought in to the front of the church and also a side table for working. A group of the youngest children began by setting the table—with tablecloth, plates, cutlery, flowers, etc.)

GRACE
Verses from Psalm 145, said together:
    All your creatures, Lord, will praise you,
    and all your people will give you thanks.
    Your rule is eternal, and you are king for ever.
    The Lord is faithful to his promises,
    and everything he does is good.
    He helps those who are in trouble;
    he lifts those who have fallen.
    All living things look hopefully to you,
    and you give them food when they need it.
    You give them enough and satisfy the needs of all.
    I will always praise the Lord;
    let all his creatures praise his holy name for ever.

SOUP
>The story of Esau and Jacob.
>>*(Short talk, including the story from Genesis.)*

>Lentil Soup
>>*(The ingredients put in a pot: Comment about how this story pointed forward to God's purposes for his people.)*

>Lord's Prayer
>>West Indian setting, sung together.

MAIN COURSE
>Food, then and now.
>>*(Question and answer with the children about favourite foods. Short talk about food in Biblical times . . . meat for very special occasions.)*

>Reading
>>Luke 15 : 20-24.
>>>*(Read by Sunday School child.)*

>The fatted calf
>>*(A large piece of red meat shown. Comment on the Prodigal, celebration and God's will for everyone to share.)*

>Hymn 413
>>'Jesus shall reign'
>>>*(Comment about the situation of the hungry, our luxury and Christian Aid.)*

>Prayer for others
>>To the words: 'For these we would pray' congregation responds: 'Lord, hear our prayer.'

>Song
>>'The Family of Man'

DESSERT
> Reading
>> Numbers 13:20-27.
>>> *(Read by a Sunday School child.)*

> Fruit
>> *(Bowl of fruit produced, with Jaffa orange from the Holy Land. Comment on the Christian hope of the final fulfilment of God's purposes when the whole world will be a promised land.)*

An Affirmation of Faith, said together:
> We believe that people
>> of all ages and countries and colours
>> have been made to live together
>> in peace and harmony
>> as one human family.

> We believe that the things that destroy people
>> and tear them apart—
>> greed, hatred, violence—
>> will finally be shown to be less strong than love.

> We believe in Jesus
>> who came to show us how people can live together,
>> who died to overcome evil
>> and lives to prove the power of love.

> Because of what we know about Jesus, we believe in God:
>> with the whole Church, we honour him.
>> With the help of his Spirit
>> we shall do all we can
>> to care for others and to live as his family.
>> AMEN.

>>> *(This statement was framed by a planning group in connection with another service.)*

Offering brought forward.

Prayer of Dedication, said together:

> Living God, with these our gifts, we dedicate our-
> selves again to your service. Forgive our lack of
> concern for our brothers and sisters who are hun-
> gry. Increase our sympathy and expand our vision
> of your purposes. Inspire us to work, with love,
> for justice and peace, in the joy and strength of
> Jesus Christ our Saviour.   AMEN.

Hymn

> 'Praise and Thanksgiving'

Benediction

BREAD AND CHEESE LUNCH

*(The congregation moved to the hall for a simple lunch,
donating the price of a full meal to Christian Aid.)*

5.   A FAMILY SERVICE FOR HARVEST

A spotlight plays on the harvest display.

PRAYER (with eyes open)

When the opening music ends, the minister, out of sight and using a microphone (or speaking from behind the congregation) invites the people to look towards the harvest offering. The thanksgiving prayer in *Worship Now,* p. 195 could be used.

HYMN

READINGS (suitably introduced)

Genesis 1 : 24-31 or Job 28 : 1-11
Luke 12 : 15-21.

PRAYER—of Confession

Worship Now, p. 194 would be suitable.

THE HARVEST ROUND

The congregation is divided into three or four groups: the tune is Three Blind Mice.

'Praise his name, praise his name,
He sends the wind, he sends the rain;
He sends the cold and then the heat
To ripen every grain of wheat
That everyone will have bread to eat and
Praise his name.'

TALK

Centred on the vegetable used by families in some parts of Africa when other foods have run out. Its name is *sukumu wiki* which means 'pushing through the week'. (See *New Internationalist,* No. 42, p. 10.)

HYMN

'Now join we to praise our creator.' (Tune: 'Red River Valley'.) *New Church Praise,* No. 71. Abridged version and tune in *Faith, Folk and Festivity.*

NEWS AND INTIMATIONS

BRINGING OUR OWN HARVEST

The congregation are now invited to stand by groups in their places (and to remain standing) as the offering of the harvest particular to them is mentioned—e.g.: 'The second group represents all those who make things: will members of this group please stand'—followed by a single sentence of thanksgiving and petition in each case.

A simplified version of that in *Celebration,* Book 1, pp. 38-39, was used.

All then resume their seats.

OFFERING

PRAYERS—of Intercession etc., and Lord's Prayer.

HYMN

BENEDICTION

BIBLIOGRAPHY

General Books about Worship

Dom Gregory Dix, *The shape of the liturgy,* Dacre Press.

J. G. Davies (ed.), *A Dictionary of Liturgy and Worship,* SCM, 1972.

Charles Davis, *Body as Spirit: The Nature of Religious Feeling,* Hodder and Stoughton, 1976.

Frank Glendinning (ed.), *The Church and the Arts,* SCM, 1960.

James, Wainright and Yarnold, *The Study of Liturgy,* SPCK, 1978.

Jasper and Cumming, *Prayers of the Eucharist, Early and Reformed,* Collins, 1975.

Raimundo Panikkar, *Worship and Secular Man,* Darton Longman and Todd, 1973.

Erik Routley, *Words, Music and the Church,* Herbert Jenkins, 1968, and other titles.

J. J. von Allmen, *Worship, Its Theology and Practice,* Lutterworth, 1965.

Geoffrey Wainright, *Doxology: the Praise of God in Worship, Doctrine and Life,* Epworth, 1980.

(smaller books and pamphlets)

J. M. Ross, *Four Centuries of Scottish Worship,* St. Andrew Press, 1972.

Learning Together about Christian Worship, Committee on Public Worship and Aids to Devotion, 1974.

The Lord's Supper and the Children of the Church, Committee on Parish Education, 1979.

Weekly Communion in the Church of Scotland, Committee on Public Worship and Aids to Devotion.

Worship, Issues for the Church 2, St. Andrew Press, 1973.

New Forms of Worship

J. G. Davies, *New Perspectives on Worship Today,* SCM, 1978.

Colin Hodgetts, *Exploring Worship: a Group Study Guide,* Mowbrays, 1980.

R. C. D. Jasper (ed.), *Getting the Liturgy Right: Practical Liturgical Principles for Today,* SPCK, 1980.

John Killinger, *Leave it to the Spirit: a Handbook for Experimental Worship,* SCM, 1971.

ANNE LONG, *Praise Him in the Dance: a Practical Guide for Drama and Dance,* Hodder and Stoughton, 1976.

MICHAEL TAYLOR, *Variations on a Theme: some Guidelines for Everyday Christians who want to Reform the Liturgy,* Galliard, 1973.

Resources for Worship

The Book of Common Order 1979, St. Andrew Press.

Prayers for Sunday Services (companion volume to above), 1980.

Prayers for Contemporary Worship, St. Andrew Press, 1977.

The Daily Office (Revised) R. C. D. JASPER (ed.), SPCK, 1978.

EDMUND BANYARD, *Word Alive,* Belton Books, 1969.

EDMUND BANYARD, *News Extra,* Galliard, 1971.

CAIRNS, PITT-WATSON, WHYTE and HONEYMAN, *Worship Now,* St. Andrew Press, 1972.

CAMPLING and DAVIS, *Words for Worship,* Edward Arnold, 1969.

ALAN GAUNT, *New Prayers for Worship: with Supplements,* John Paul, The Preachers' Press.

EDMUND JONES, *Worship and Wonder,* Galliard, 1971.

CARYL MICKLEM, *Contemporary Prayers for Public Worship,* SCM, 1967.

CARYL MICKLEM, *More Contemporary Prayers,* SCM, 1970.

'Risk', vol. 11, Nos. 2-3, 1973, "A Worship Book for the Fifth Assembly of the World Council of Churches".

Recent Collections of Hymns and Songs

BRALEY, PRATT GREEN, PERCIVAL and COLEMAN (ed.), *Partners in Praise,* Stainer and Bell, and Methodist Division of Education and Youth, 1979.

WCC, *Cantate Domino,* Bärenreiter, 1974.

COLVIN and MCLEAN (ed.), *Free to Serve: Hymns from Africa,* Iona Community.

COLVIN and GALBRAITH (ed.), *Leap My Soul: More Hymns from Africa,* Iona Community.

DAMIAN LUNDY (ed.), *Songs of the Spirit,* Mayhew-McCrimmon, 1978.

KEVIN MAYHEW, *20th Century Folk Hymnal* (four volumes), Mayhew-McCrimmon.

New Church Praise (United Reformed Church), St. Andrew Press, 1975. (Hymn book supplements are also published by other major denominations.)

New Ways to Praise (provisional title): a supplement to *Church Hymnary: Third Edition*, 1981.

PULKINGHAM and HARPER, *Sound of Living Waters/Fresh Sounds* (combined volume), Hodder and Stoughton, 1978.

PETER SMITH (ed.), *Faith, Folk and Clarity; Faith, Folk and Nativity; Faith, Folk and Festivity;* Galliard.

PETER SMITH (ed.), *Jesus Folk*, Galliard.

Records

Word (UK) Ltd., Northbridge Road, Berkhamstead, Herts. will send a complete catalogue ranging from contemporary rock to traditional Gospel music.

"A star whispered", Pilgrim Records, and other titles.

"Young folk in worship", BBC Records, and other titles.

"Fourpence a day", Galliard Ltd., and other titles.

"The Sound of Celebration" (Sanctus), from Rev. Colin Williamson, 52 Pilrig Street, Edinburgh EH6 5AS.

"Songs for the seventies—and beyond", (Emmaus Road Band), St. Andrew Press Cassette.

NOTE: the AVA unit of the Church of Scotland, 121 George Street, Edinburgh EH2 4YN can provide tapes, slides, films and other useful aids.

ACKNOWLEDGEMENTS

A volume such as this naturally contains quotations, echoes and reflections from other publications in the same field. The compilers acknowledge their wide-ranging indebtedness and trust that there has been no infringement of copyright.

Thanks are due to the following for permission to use material as noted:

Stainer & Bell Ltd. for 'Let us affirm our desire' (p. 101) from *Worship and Wonder* (ed. E. S. P. Jones) and 'Let's play a game' (p. 111) by Malcolm Stewart, from *Jesus Folk*.

Galliard for 'When in his own image' (p. 106) by Fred Kaan.

The World Council of Churches for 'Evening Litany' (p. 55) from *Risk*, vol. 11, Nos. 2-3, and for the acclamation 'Raise us up from fear. . .' on p. 99 by Dieter Trautwein.

The Paulist Press for 'We beseech you. . .' (p. 36) from *Your Word is Near* by Huub Oosterhuis, ©The Paulist Press.

The Saint Andrew Press for the dialogue 'Who are you. . .' (p. 24) by Edmund Jones from *Worship Now*.

SPCK for permission to reproduce the prayers in the Pentecost Service (pp. 98, 99, 100) from *The Daily Office Revised* ©The Joint Liturgical Group.